Praise for *The People Principle*

"*The People Principle* shows with practical advice and sound concepts how we can all develop the potential of others, and find joy in doing so. Ron Willingham, in his typical straightforward way, shouts the truth that our endeavors will only succeed if we first focus on growing successful people."

—Marvin Girouard, President and
Chief Operating Officer of Pier 1 Imports

"*The People Principle* is a powerful, thought-provoking, and comprehensive look at how a company can get the most out of its most precious resources: its employees. This should be required reading for all managers."

—Geoffrey Brewer, Executive Editor
of *Sales & Marketing Management*

"No matter whether you have two employees on your payroll or one thousand, management consultant Ron Willingham has motivational tips to impart to you in *The People Principle*."

—*Publishers Weekly*

The
People
Principle

A Revolutionary Redefinition
of Leadership

Ron Willingham

ST. MARTIN'S GRIFFIN 🅜 NEW YORK

Design by Nancy Resnick

Library of Congress Cataloging-in-Publication Data

Willingham, Ron.
  The people principle : A revolutionary redefinition of leadership / Ron Willingham.
    p.   cm.
   ISBN 0-312-16871-3 (hc)
   ISBN 0-312-24490-8 (pbk)
   1. Employee motivation. I. Title.
HF5549.5.M63W55 1997
658.3'14—dc21   97-14650
                                                                 CIP

20 19 18 17 16 15 14 13 12 11

The master Beethoven, able to put the same art in words that he did in his time-honored music, wrote, "From the glow of enthusiasm I let the melody escape. I pursue it. Breathlessly I catch up with it. It flies again, it disappears, it plunges into a chaos of diverse emotions. I catch it again, I seize it. I embrace it with delight . . . I multiply it by modulation, and at last I triumph in the first theme. There is the whole symphony."

Mere sheets of music, though, do not a symphony make. Beautiful music becomes the congruent product of artists who master their own roles under the direction of a skilled conductor.

A highly productive and profitable organization is like a beautiful symphony. It brings together instruments of talent, knowledge, experience, skills, values, and goals that when played in harmony produce the beautiful music of profitability and productivity. All the elements can only reach their full range of artistic excellence at the hands of a skillful conductor—a leader.

A leader who knows how to help people become *their best*.

Certainly art, so far as we can judge of it, has not yet discovered in this darkness what it is that holds all men together and could give expression to their psychic wholeness.

—CARL JUNG

Contents

The People Principle

People have unlimited potential that has been largely unrecognized and untapped. When discovered and accessed, this potential can lead them to far greater levels of productivity than they ever imagined, causing them to feel better about themselves and enjoy life more.

The Law of Limited Performance

People soon discover the level of performance their managers will settle for, and then gravitate to that level. Managers then assume that's all that people are capable of achieving, so they accept it as fact and quit challenging their people to get better. So, both reinforce what the other believes.

Introduction

What is the People Principle?

It's simply this: *People are more important than processes.* Processes don't produce, people do. Processes don't think, feel, or create. People do. Before processes can improve, people must improve.

In the last decade, organizations have spent billions on process improvement and reorganization; and where are they now?

In chaos. Low employee morale. Decreased productivity. Workplaces filled with fear, distrust, and paranoia. The prevailing message has been sent loud and clear—profits and processes are more important than people.

It is a crisis that you, I, and our children will pay for dearly. We'll pay with lower standards of living, with tarnished career satisfaction, and with diminished quality of life.

In my opinion, flat productivity is the greatest business crisis in the world right now.

Why have the billions spent on technology and organizational strategies not worked? It's painfully simple. They focused too much on processes and overlooked the productive potential of people. People aren't machines; they aren't even logical most of the time. They don't produce simply because they have been so commanded. No, people are 85 percent emotional beings and 15 percent logical beings. So with most management strategies today, organizations are getting a fraction of the potential of people depending on the insight and people skills of managers.

To increase significantly productivity in the tough years ahead, leaders and managers must learn about and maximize this incredibly vast, yet latent, pool of potential in their people, a pool that's currently unchallenged and untapped.

They will have no other choice!

But most managers aren't trained to know how to plug in to the powerfully creative dimensions of human potential. They know about numbers, budgets—logical stuff—but very few are prepared for the important role of building people. A few do it naturally; most don't.

Hence this book—understanding how to create the proper environment so people discover and actualize more of their vast creative potential and approach their jobs with more joy and productivity. It's here that managers will see significant increases in the bottom line while at the same time experiencing more harmonious work environments and higher employee satisfaction and loyalty. This in turn will prepare the foundation for stronger customer satisfaction and loyalty.

This book is aimed at the greatest single need in organizations today—*how to help people become their best*. The concepts are sound, practical, and workable. They are the fruit of the experience I've gained from having over 1.5 million people in over two thousand different organizations around the world go through my training courses.

The principles we developed transcend culture and languages. They address the most basic needs people have and, when filled, lead them on to greater self-fulfillment, productivity, and job satisfaction.

Although I have cast these concepts in organizational settings, they work for anyone who wants to help people become their best—parents, coaches, teachers, friends.

You'll see that as soon as you get into it.

So, thanks for picking up this book. I'm honored. Read the chapters and practice the action guides that I'll lay out and you'll see significant increases in your people's growth.

Let me hear from you.

Ron Willingham
Integrity Systems
2425 E. Camelback Road, Suite 785
Phoenix, AZ 85016
602-955-9090
602-955-1212 (fax)
inten phx@aol.com

People have an innate need to be valued and to know that they count for something. They need to feel that you don't just see them as a bunch of social security numbers showing up for work!

1. "I'll Work My Butt Off for You!"

Few things help an individual more than to place responsibility upon him and let him know that you trust him.

—BOOKER T. WASHINGTON

John had just been through our Manager's Coaching and Counseling Training with National Car Rental in a Florida city. He was a manager in one of their New York offices. After completing the training he had a visit with one of his people, a man we'll call Archie. Archie was a fourteen-year veteran of that office and widely known for being uncooperative. He was, to be as positive as possible, undistinguished. In fact he was on probation at that time.

Very shortly, John called Archie into his office for a coaching session as our people had taught him to do. Well aware of his reputation, Archie not only dreaded the session but considered the possibility that he might be terminated.

John began their conversation by telling Archie that he appreciated his long-term employment, specifically pointing out a few strengths he had observed. After mentioning these positive traits and actions, John told him that there were some things that needed attention in his work. John assured him that these could be easily worked through and emphasized his value to the operation.

Shocked by the positive tone he heard, Archie was in disbelief. He said, "John, when you called me in, I thought you were going to fire me. I've been with National fourteen years," he went on, "and this is the *first* time I've ever been told that I've done something right and that I'm appreciated!"

Pausing for a moment, he then looked into John's eyes and said, "I haven't been working as hard as I should have, but . . . I want you to know . . . that from now on . . . I'll work my butt off for you!"

And he did.

Within a year John promoted Archie. He'd earned it by changing from negative to positive. From a "goof-off" to a "go-getter."

What happened? Did John give him a new computer or some other advanced technology? Did Archie learn new product or industry knowledge?

No!

Analyze what John did with Archie. It's amazingly simple. He believed in him.

1. He valued him.

2. He chose to recognize his contributions, although it would have been very easy to focus on his many shortcomings.

3. He looked for, discovered, and pointed out strengths he saw in him.

4. He was up-front and honest about some problem areas but communicated his belief that they could be worked out.

5. He listened to him.

6. He let him know that he cared about him as a person.

It would have been easy for John to do just the opposite—to call Archie in and give him the "shape up or ship out" speech, to revisit his probationary status, or even to terminate him.

But, he didn't! Instead, he not only maximized an asset that they'd invested in heavily, but he helped transform a person's life.

In a sense, John held the power in his hands either to build or destroy Archie. At that time, the very future of a person and a family rested in the balance, either to be saved or gutted. John's values, beliefs, and skills all came together to help a person and to increase his company's productivity and profitability by positively building his people.

That's what this book is about:

- increasing your organization's productivity and profitability by building your people.

- looking at people and seeing them not as they *are* but as they *can become*.

- seeing more in people than they see in themselves.

- convincing people of their greatness.

- helping people climb out of their limited, self-imposed "areas of the possible" to develop new, expanded internal belief systems, thus moving them onto higher levels of productivity.

It's about being the kind of person that others want to follow, about strong values, ethics, integrity, and authenticity. It's about believing so strongly in people that their awareness of your belief in them causes them to rise to new heights of individual growth and achievement.

It's about getting people to say, "I'll work my butt off for you!"

Leadership Ingredients and That "Something Else"

Leadership is the sum of its parts—and something else. This "something else" is variable—it manifests itself differently for different people in different life situations, yet it's essentially the same common ingredient.

In this book, I'll share with you some of the parts of leadership. These are specific skills, behaviors, attitudes, and ways of thinking. Developing these will enhance your leadership skills but will not necessarily make you a leader. To become a leader you must develop these skills, behaviors, and thinking patterns *and* discover for yourself that "something else."

In these pages I'll lead you through ideas and suggested actions that, if you'll follow, will develop your leadership traits. I will not, however, attempt to tell you directly what that "something else" is. I will hint at it and occasionally drop clues, but I will not share it directly. It must be up to you to discover it for yourself so that it can become yours—in your own life, where you are, with your own values, within the sets of opportunities that you'll create for yourself. When you discover it, you'll know it by the fresh new exhilaration, energy, and sense of fulfillment you'll suddenly enjoy. You'll also know it by your people's positive response and belief in you.

I can only tell you that this "something else" is the chemical ingredient that bonds skills and abilities together to multiply their effectiveness. It is the catalyst that, when added to the other ingredients, causes something new and more powerful to be achieved.

This "something else" isn't intellectually taught; it's experientially discovered. It does not evolve out of our rational, conscious, cognitive, logical, linear world. It functions on a much deeper creative level. It's not gained by education; it's granted as a process of indirection, a serendipity. It mysteriously appears, unsought, as we seek certain other goals of growth and learning.

But, that's enough about this secret of leadership for now—except to say that if you're searching and open to discovery, you'll stumble over it numerous times in this book. Depending on your quest for wisdom, your desire to learn and willingness to practice the action guides I'll lay out for you, you'll either come face-to-face with it, or it'll sail over your head unnoticed.

Values, Beliefs, Skills

How often does the very future of a person like Archie rest in your hands? How often do your decisions and actions influence the direction of someone's life? How do you emotionally deal with this awesome responsibility—the responsibility for a person's future?

That person's life could go one way or another depending on your actions and decisions. It's an incredibly sobering thought, isn't it?

I believe the very future of organizations rests in their leaders' ability to help people become their best. This means that they must nurture, challenge, and build people. They have to select the right people, be able to see potential in each person, then bring out this hidden value. This involves leadership skills that are consistent with a few core values and beliefs.

Let's think more about these core values and beliefs.

Effective Leadership Begins with a Fundamental Belief

The more I learn about leadership and the more I attempt to become a more effective leader, the more I'm convinced that it all begins with a fundamental belief. And this one foundational belief is this:

    All people have unlimited potential that has been largely unrecognized and untapped. When discovered and accessed, this potential can lead them to far greater levels of productivity than they ever imagined, causing them to feel better about themselves and enjoy life more.

Now, stop a moment and read this statement again.

Do you believe this? Not only intellectually or conceptually but down-in-your-gut viscerally? Would you stake your leadership future on it?

It's always been this way. You're probably where you are today because someone held this fundamental belief and then went about helping you discover and actualize abilities you didn't know you had.

Leaders' Beliefs Often Become Self-Fulfilling Prophecies

Over thirty years ago a friend, Joe Barnett, expressed a belief in me that totally changed my life.

For six years I had owned a small furniture and decorating business that, because of a deep local economic downturn, was going down the tubes.

Joe, a minister who had just moved to town, was sharp, articulate, and motivated. We became close friends immediately. Finally, after being in denial about my problem for several months, I was at the end of my rope and had to talk to someone and do something. When I told him about my situation, he reflected on some self-help books that both of us had read and some training courses that we had attended. Like me, he was a graduate of the Dale Carnegie Course, and it had caused tremendous growth in both of our lives. I had also attended some courses sponsored by the National Retail Furniture Association.

Joe looked at me, and said, "I think you should get into training. You'd be great at it. In fact, we need someone to design a leadership development course and conduct it at our church, and I think you can do that."

Wow! I thought. *If he thinks I can do that, maybe he sees something in me that I don't see in me.*

My immediate response was, "Okay, I'll do it, if you'll help me."

The truth was that I knew absolutely nothing about training or writing. Nothing! But my insides told me that if a sharp guy like Joe Barnett thought I could do it, I must be able to do it. With his help, I put together a very homemade course and conducted it. In doing so I discovered I had natural gifts for training and writing. I don't really know how I knew what to do, I just did.

The participants in the first course I conducted experienced incredible growth. I was so pumped that I made an immediate decision to sell my store and start conducting courses full-time. Which I did. A complete transformation took place. My whole life, my internal view of myself and my goals, changed. Suddenly I was swept into an incredibly exciting life that I'd never dreamed possible.

All this happened because of the belief that Joe Barnett expressed in me.

And you know what? Almost everyone can give tribute to the transforming power of someone's belief in them. Most can trace their success back to people who saw more in them than they saw in themselves, who helped them discover their better selves and actualize this discovery into meaningful careers or actions.

I'll bet it's true for you.

"I See More in You Than You See in You."

Have you had people in your life who saw more in you than you saw in yourself?

I've asked this question to many audiences. Almost every hand goes up. Then I ask, "How many of you can say that you had more than four or five people in your life who did this?" Ninety percent of all the hands go down.

Interesting survey, isn't it? And what a tragedy that so few people exist in our lives.

How about you? How many people in your life saw more in you than you saw in yourself? And then their belief in you helped you discover what they saw in you?

Not many? Then you're average.

I remember Joe Jordan, who was the manager of a super-market where I worked my junior year in college. I earned sixty-five cents an hour—minimum wage then. Joe was a master at building people. His official title was Store Manager, but it should have been Director of Cheerleading and En-couraging and People Building.

My guess is that he spent 80 percent of his time catching people doing stuff right and then making a big deal out of it. He would walk up to where I was stocking shelves and make me feel like the whole universe had just been made a better place in which to live because of the way I was turning all the cans so the labels faced forward. And, man, you should have heard his accolades at the way I mopped the floors at night.

Joe loved to get us in front of people and brag about us. He had pet names for all the employees, especially the sack boys. All the names were "build-ups" not "put-downs."

It was one of my greatest experiences. He was an incredibly effective leader and builder of people. Everyone loved him and worked hard for him.

Joe saw greatness in people who didn't see it in themselves.

Great leaders—people who get more done through people—have learned the transforming power of belief in people's po-tential.

Leadership Beliefs and Core Values

Fundamental to effective leadership is a set of Ten Beliefs or Core Values that drive your actions, decisions, and behaviors.

1. *Leadership*—People want to be led. They don't want to be managed.

2. *Vision*—People want to know where you're going.

3. *Pride*—People want you to feel that they count for something.

4. *Congruence*—People feel right about you when they see you doing the right things.

5. *Communication*—People perform better when you're open with them and listen to their concerns and ideas.

6. *Trust*—People need to know that you'll be fair and consistent.

7. *Character*—People will ultimately find out and be influenced by what you're made of.

8. *Responsibility*—People feel better about you and themselves when you cause them to make and keep commitments.

9. *Integrity*—People will respect you when they see that what you preach is what you practice.

10. *Wisdom*—People will learn most from you when they see you temper your knowledge with good judgment and concern for others.

On a following page is a personal assessment for you to score yourself in the ten beliefs and values. You may even want to photocopy it and ask four or five associates to score you. If you do, please ask them to score you anonymously and give the assessments back to you. It's important that you don't know who scores you and that they know that you won't know. Otherwise, they'll probably skew their responses and not be totally honest. Of course, you need their honesty if the assessment is going to help.

Look at each trait and its description. Ask yourself, "How well do I fill this need that people have?" Ask, "To what extent do my actions show that I subscribe to this value or belief?" If

Leadership Beliefs and Core Values Assessment

1. *Leadership*—People want to be led. They don't want to be managed.

1	2	3	4	5	6	7	8	9	10
Never									Always

2. *Vision*—People want to know where you're going.

1	2	3	4	5	6	7	8	9	10

3. *Pride*—People want you to feel that they count for something.

1	2	3	4	5	6	7	8	9	10

4. *Congruence*—People feel right about you when they see you doing the right things.

1	2	3	4	5	6	7	8	9	10

5. *Communication*—People perform better when you're open with them and listen to their concerns and ideas.

1	2	3	4	5	6	7	8	9	10

6. *Trust*—People need to know that you'll be fair and consistent.

1	2	3	4	5	6	7	8	9	10

7. *Character*—People will ultimately find out and be influenced by what you're made of.

1	2	3	4	5	6	7	8	9	10

8. *Responsibility*—People feel better about you and themselves when you cause them to make and keep commitments.

1	2	3	4	5	6	7	8	9	10

9. *Integrity*—People will respect you when they see that what you preach is what you practice.

1	2	3	4	5	6	7	8	9	10

10. *Wisdom*—People will learn most from you when they see you temper your knowledge with good judgment and concern for others.

1	2	3	4	5	6	7	8	9	10

After scoring yourself in each of these ten traits, connect your dots and form a vertical graph.

it's *never* descriptive, place a dot at 1. If it's *always* descriptive, place a dot at 10, or wherever in between that you think honestly describes your actual behaviors.

Values and Core Beliefs Drive Behavior

Why am I making such a big deal about values and core beliefs?

Because your values and core beliefs drive your behavior! Your *external* actions and responses will usually be congruent with your *internal* values and core beliefs. These inner beliefs about what's right and what's wrong are the foundation of your personality. They define *who* you are and how you treat other people. What you *value* reveals your *values.* Value people over processes, and they'll get that message, too. Value processes over people, and they'll get that message. Your actions, decisions, and reactions reveal your values—and, believe me, people figure them out very quickly.

A decade ago I couldn't talk to corporate executives about values. Many would have thought that I was an evangelist or trying to convert them to some cultish way of thinking. Fortunately, as change accelerated in the nineties they began to look deeper into what causes human action, and when they looked they discovered that people are multidimensional beings whose major motivation is to seek congruence between what they do and who they are. The more congruent they become, the healthier and more productive they'll be.

Jerry Colangelo, head of the Phoenix Suns, Arizona Rattlers, and Arizona Diamondbacks, is without a doubt the most influential person in Arizona. No one has done more to rebuild downtown Phoenix than he has.

A man of impeccable integrity, he has strong beliefs about the need for high ethics and values in business, industry, and yes, even politics. "We have gotten so caught up in building and growing and expanding . . . and the cutthroat business that it's out there, we have lost focus," he said.

"Things used to be a certain way, where there was a real

value system," he added. "But I think there is a current read-justment to stronger ethics and values, refocusing; because it became evident that we were missing that. I do think that they're on the upswing."

I asked him what he looks for in people. ". . . The key word is consistency," he replied. "The probability of an unstable person being successful is not very likely, so, you know, how a person treats his wife and kids in public and at home is probably how he's going to treat his customer or business associates."

"How are ethics communicated?" I asked. "Can they be taught?"

He replied, "I think the best way to teach ethics is by observation. By setting an example. And that starts at the top. How a leader conducts himself. How he treats people. How he values every association. That tunnels through any organization.

"I think," he continued, "that positive morals and values can be enhanced in seminars and courses—by creating awareness."

Reflecting a moment, he added, "I want to believe and do believe, that people are basically good. They need to be reminded of that sometimes."

Here is an extremely strong individual. Attempting to analyze some of the factors that contribute to his strength, I was struck with the powerful congruence within him. Harmony between his beliefs, his practices, his concern for people, his massive contributions to our city, his strong religious faith, his intense drive to get big things done, and his willingness to shoulder huge risks.

He ended the interview by summarizing his feelings like this: "I've seen a lot of great people come and go, and it's interesting that we've talked about ethics and morality and values. There is no question that those who have all of that in proper perspective and have their life in order, have a much greater chance to fully develop as a leader. And those who do not have their life in order, quite often fall short in terms of becoming a leader. Again, it's the consistency. It's who you are. It's not an act. It's not a game. I look for people who have their act together, who are really consistent, because you just don't want to be associated with those who aren't."

Do strong ethics and values impact productivity? This is an incredibly important question for every manager to ask and answer.

In the seventies and eighties, managers thought they could fix flat productivity with technology. And who can blame them considering all the incredible advances in computers, PCs, fax machines, cellular telephones, and a plethora of other marvelous inventions. Many managers clearly valued technology over people. Their silent message was loudly heard: "We'll invest millions in technology, but we don't see much value in investing in your personal growth!"

Technology depersonalized many job functions, which left people, needing social contact and relationships, feeling a loss of meaning in their jobs. The "High Tech/High Touch" phenomenon that John Naisbitt wrote about in his landmark book *Megatrends* escaped the comprehension of many managers. This favoritism for technology contributed to the flattening of productivity that, according to Andersen Consulting, increased only 1 percent from 1982 to 1992.

Addressing the human spirit—understanding people's needs to experience meaning and security in their jobs—was overlooked as managers stood in awe of the rapid technology that was constantly making last month's models obsolete.

It had to shift. As people search for greater significance, they move more toward the intrinsic needs that are at their core. They begin to look for authentic people they can trust, follow, believe, and respect. I am totally convinced that we are seeing and will continue to see, a paradigm shift wherein managers' ability to lead people will depend on their values and respect for people. I believe that leaders whose decisions and responses are driven by strong, positive values and beliefs will naturally empower people to greater productivity.

I'll weave this belief throughout this book.

People Produce More When Managers' Actions Are Driven by Strong, Positive Values

Dr. Herbert Benson of Harvard Medical School makes some significant cases for strong values and core beliefs in his book *Timeless Healing*. Using the research he and his associates did, he asserts that people with strong values physically heal faster than others. He also writes, and notice this, that people heal faster when their caregivers live out strong, positive values. Not only did Dr. Benson prove by scientific experiments that strong values influence healing, but he also proved that patients heal faster when:

1. The doctor or caregiver believes in the efficacy of the treatment being recommended.
2. When the patient believes in the efficacy of the treatment, and
3. When rapport, trust and respect exist between the caregiver and patients.

Think about that for a moment. What's the message for leaders?

Parallel to Dr. Benson's findings here are some discoveries I've made that relate to leadership and employee productivity. First, productivity increases when managers espouse and exhibit strong, positive values. Second, it increases when their people espouse and exhibit strong, positive values.

In addition, employee satisfaction and loyalty, customer satisfaction and loyalty increase when:

1. Leaders or managers understand and buy into the organization's mission, purpose, and core values and when their actions are congruent with them.
2. Employees understand and buy into the mission, purpose,

and core values of the organization and when their actions are congruent with them.

3. When rapport, trust, and mutual respect exist between managers and employees.

I'll get into this more in the next chapter, but I wanted to emphasize this vital point here.

What Are Your Core Beliefs and Values?

As we have thought about values and core beliefs, how would you define yours? If you and I were sitting talking and I asked you what your values and beliefs about people are, what would you tell me? How would you shape them into words?

If I were to ask your people about your values and core beliefs, what would they tell me?

I suggest that you take a few days and think about the questions I've just asked you. Talk to your spouse, friends, mentors, or trusted advisors about them.

Come to some decision about your own values and core beliefs and write them down. When you get them written, define what behaviors, actions, or responses they will motivate.

This activity is the foundation for the growth and development that I'll guide you through in this book.

Are Ethics Good for Business?

That's a good question, isn't it? Are ethical, value-driven behaviors good for business?

Michael Roth, Chairman and CEO of Mutual of New York, believes they are. In a recent speech to the Economic Club of Phoenix, he made his case in no uncertain terms. First, he cited a recent poll of four hundred salespeople, 98 percent of whom replied that they would do anything it takes to get the sale.

"This unethical behavior is pervasive, it's alarming, and, if maintained, it's bad for business. The biggest challenge today for business," he went on, "is how to change this because good ethics means good business."

Roth emphasized that solving the problem of unethical behavior begins at the top, with an imperative for ethical practices from senior management. "It's a top-down message," he said. "The CEO must be involved, be the role model, and establish that good ethical behavior is not an option . . . it is a necessity."

Roth believes that companies can make the numbers while doing the right thing. I agree. I think strong ethical standards are good for business. It makes for greater harmony and congruence—thus creating higher employee satisfaction, ultimately higher customer satisfaction, and, most importantly, customer loyalty.

A number of years ago, my associates and I installed our *Integrity Selling®* program at about nine hundred Chevrolet dealers. There were dealers with all kinds of ethics—most were honest, highly ethical ones; others weren't. The first pilot group of twelve dealers increased their closing ratios 25 percent and their gross profit in sales 31 percent.

What caused those increases? We simply injected a new customer-focused method of selling. Rather than attempting to sell someone whatever kind of car they seemed to want to buy, we trained the salespeople and managers to take time to understand customers' needs and then honestly show them the best vehicle for their individual needs.

This customer-focused sales approach made customers feel valued and comfortable. It created trust and rapport between them and the salespeople, and they were willing to pay more in order to do business with someone they trusted.

It wasn't the strategy that made the difference; it was the motivation of the salespeople. When their main goal was to put people at ease, identify their needs, and understand how they would use a vehicle, then demonstrate one that was right in price and features, sales went up.

It was a value, not a strategy; an ethically driven practice, not a sales gimmick.

Are ethics good for business? They are if you're looking at your organization's strength and long-term success.

What This Book Is About

In this book, I'll share with you the traits, skills, attitudes, and behaviors necessary for getting more done through people. Not only will I present them, but I'll also lay out action steps that will help you learn and grow.

But, let me warn you—simply knowing the information intellectually will do you little good. In fact, it can be frustrating if you only deal with this information *intellectually* and not *experientially*. My objective is to give you a road map to leadership growth and then to get you assimilating some basic skills into your life behaviors.

Let me stop a moment and be honest and admit that you probably already know all the ideas I'll present *intellectually*. If you're just "idea surfing," then it may be a waste of your time to read this. But if you look at leadership growth as a continuum—where you never reach perfection; you simply keep learning and growing—then you'll assimilate and apply my ideas, gradually developing stronger automatic *habits* and *behaviors*.

In the decade of the nineties, when individual productivity plummeted, companies spent billions on reorganization. In at least half of the cases, it created far greater problems than it solved. The cure became more deadly than the disease. It was like using radiation to treat athlete's foot.

Throughout history, when productivity flattened or lagged and managers didn't know what to do next, they reorganized! That strategy usually takes the heat off senior managers (and their lackluster performances) and buys them time either to figure out what's wrong or string things out until retirement.

In the meantime, personal production still lags.

The Roman general Petronius said it well in 60 B.C. He wrote, "We trained hard, but it seemed that every time we were beginning to form up into teams, we were reorganized. I was to learn, later in life, that we tend to meet any new situation by reorganization; and a wonderful method it can be for creating the illusion of progress, while producing confusion, inefficiency, and demoralization."

The corporate restructuring of the 1990s had many casualties. Not because it was wrong to reorganize, because in most cases reorganization was needed. It failed because it dealt with logic and failed to consider people's emotions. It didn't address the fear, anxiety, paranoia, and emotional devastation that ensued. The factors that had caused the organizations to become strong, healthy, and productive in the first place were violated. Factors like: trust, common values, exciting missions and purposes, team synergy, and security.

Managers thought if they gave people the best tools, equipment, processes, or technology that they'd be productive. They completely overlooked the emotional ramifications. In my opinion, this is one of the biggest organizational mistakes in modern history. Senior managers were so enamored with all the new technology and organizational strategies that they forgot the human element of the equation.

Much of the corporate reorganization of the nineties made a very clear statement: People aren't as important as organizational structure. The cuts and slashes made by senior managers made a powerful statement about corporate values. Employees were left with little doubt about what senior managers' *values* were and how much the rank and file were *valued*. Morale plummeted with job security.

Today's leaders must fix this fracture. They must mend and heal by creating new organizational structures that are built on trust, common values, and mutual respect. They must get back to the root of productive, profitable organizations—well-trained, happy, productive *people*.

Organizations don't produce; people do! When organizational structure itself becomes more important than the people within it, trouble inevitably lies ahead. Organizational structure is only significant to the extent that it provides an environment in which people can work with purpose, dignity, security, creativity, and significance. Organizational structure and theory are logical, but people are emotional, not always driven by logic.

This book is about people—how to better understand, challenge, communicate with, lead, inspire them. How to see more potential in them than they see in themselves. How to create an environment in which they can discover the vast, untapped potential within themselves and actualize it into on-the-job efficiency and productivity. Bottom line, it's how to help people do their best.

Summing Up

People have an innate need to know that they are valued. They need their work to have meaning.

Leaders who exhibit strong, positive values in their lives enable their people to be more productive. People's job performances are influenced by their leaders' beliefs. I mentioned a Fundamental Belief about People, the People Principle, that when managers embrace and practice it, it empowers people to reach higher levels of productivity.

> All people have unlimited potential that has been largely unrecognized and untapped that when discovered and accessed can lead them to far greater levels of productivity than they ever imagined, causing them to feel better about themselves and enjoy life more.

I've often noticed that leaders' beliefs about people become self-fulfilling prophecies. People unconsciously pick up their manager's beliefs in them and react accordingly. This should be sufficient cause for any thinking person to choose carefully the thoughts he or she selects to think about others.

Great leaders have the ability to see more in people than

people see in themselves and then help them discover and actualize their potential in their lives.

The ten-statement assessment will help you evaluate some important leadership beliefs and core values that impact your leadership effectiveness.

Your own core values and beliefs about people motivate your actions, responses, and behaviors. What you value becomes who you are and influences what you do.

How to Get the Most from This Book

There are three types of readers of self-help books.

1. People who pick them up and read the first couple of chapters, put them down, and never go back.
2. People who read them through completely and put them on a shelf.
3. People who read them this way:
   a. Read the whole book to understand its scope. Then go back and spend a week reading a chapter at a time.
   b. Underline key ideas and make notes in the page margins.
   c. Scan the chapter during the week to refresh their memories.
   d. Take action and practice the key ideas in their daily lives.
   e. Evaluate how well they practiced the key ideas.

Follow the ideas in #3 above and you'll get the most from this book.

Organizations everywhere are consistently searching for people to whom they can *pay* lots of money for taking responsibility and getting things done through people.

2. "I'll Pay More for This Trait Than Any Other."

The person who gets the most satisfactory results is not always the one with the most brilliant single mind, but rather the one who can best co-ordinate the brains and talents of his associates.

—W. ALTON JONES

Here's an ad that, in a sense, constantly appears in newspapers, trade journals, and other business publications around the world.

Wanted
Someone to Take Responsibility
for
Getting Things Done Through People.
Salary range from $50,000 to $10,000,000 per year
depending on your ability to get results.
Apply in Person.
Please hurry!
We need you badly!

Think I'm exaggerating? Check it out for yourself. Look in the *Wall Street Journal*. Look in newspapers in Stockholm, Sydney, Singapore, São Paulo, or Syracuse. Ask high-rolling headhunters what kind of people they're looking for and what organizations are willing to pay if they find the right person.

Ask yourself, "Why was Chrysler willing to pay Iacocca several million dollars per year? Why will a basketball team pay a winning coach $7,000,000 a year and more?"

It's very simple. The pay reflects their willingness to assume total responsibility for getting results. Yeah, it's that simple. They're paid consistent with their ability to get things done— to get things done through people.

Most of us are! That's real life, although not everyone understands this law of compensation.

Real life is asking yourself the following question: "How much do I want to earn and achieve?" Then, once you've come to a realistic decision (not a pie-in-the-sky one), ask yourself this question: "Okay, if this is how much I want to earn or achieve, then what level of results will I have to take responsibility for making happen in order to earn this much?"

The third question that separates the sheep from the goats: "Am I willing to prepare myself, take action, and do this?"

You'll answer this third question with your actions. You'll make the choice. Your decisions and commitments will yield your future effects. So much of life is cause and effect, you know.

It's Always Been This Way

What I'm saying isn't new stuff. It's always been this way. Rewards follow performance. People get rewarded and compensated according to the results they cause. The rewards may be money, acclaim, self-respect, or other forms of compensation, but they follow performance. They come when you assume responsibility for results and then carry through and make them happen. As I said, it's always been this way.

In the midst of the Industrial Revolution in America, the steel baron, Andrew Carnegie, reputed richest man in the U.S., gave a man a million-dollar-a-year bonus. This was at a time when a person earning $100 per month was considered quite successful. "Why did you pay Charles Schwab a million-dollar bonus each year?" a reporter once asked Carnegie. "Because he has the ability to excite people!" Carnegie responded. "I'll pay more for that trait than for any other!"

The ability to excite people!

The same is true today. People who have the ability to excite people and lead them to higher levels of productivity are the ones who put themselves in a jet stream that propels them to higher and higher levels of success and prosperity.

Around the turn of the century Elbert Hubbard said it this way: "Initiative means doing the right thing without being told. The world bestows its big prizes, both in money and honor, for but one thing—initiative."

A few decades later a pudgy little cigar-chomping Englishman assumed the gigantic, seemingly impossible responsibility of saving a nation by saying, "We will not flag or fail. We shall go on to the end. We shall fight on the seas and oceans; we shall fight with growing confidence and growing strength in the air; we shall defend our island, whatever the cost may be, we shall fight on the beaches, we shall fight on the landing grounds; we shall fight in the fields and in the streets; we shall fight in the hills; we shall never surrender!"

His vision was clearly stated. His belief galvanized and empowered a nation to overcome incredible odds and survive, and Winston Churchill's rewards were consistent with the level of responsibility he assumed. Not necessarily in money but in the admiration and respect of millions of people who will remember him for his leadership. Payment that transcends money.

My firm, Integrity Systems®, has worked with over two thousand organizations in the last decade. Over a million employees and managers have graduated from our courses. My associates and I talk to many senior managers about where their business is and where they'd like to take it. I have yet to talk to a man-

ager in any organization who isn't in need of more people who
are "step-up-to-the-plate," take responsibility, and get things
done people!

Almost every organization that I know of is looking for results-oriented men and women who can get more done through
people. The truth is that there just aren't enough of these people to satisfy the demand.

If you agree with my belief and if you're like others with
whom I've discussed it, then you probably have the same questions they have. Like:

1. "Why aren't there more effective leaders available who can
   fill these voids in the marketplace?"
2. "What traits do effective leaders have that other people
   don't?"
3. "Can these traits be developed by people who aspire to
   greater leadership and income levels?"

My answers to these three questions are:

1. Beats me! You'd think that more people would recognize
   the vast opportunities and develop themselves to tap into
   them.
2. I'll get into an overview of these traits in a moment, then
   I'll spend the rest of this book helping you learn how to
   develop them.
3. Yes. Yes, these habits can be developed if you're willing to
   pay the price of learning, hard work, and personal growth.

Prepare Yourself to Take Advantage of Opportunities

Abraham Lincoln once said, "I'll prepare myself and be ready
for opportunities as they come." It's been my experience that
opportunities follow preparation. When you're prepared, op-

portunity always seems to be just around the corner. Without preparation, opportunities usually go unrecognized. "When the student is ready, the teacher appears."

As you look into the future, you can follow these steps to prepare yourself for the opportunities that will come your way.

1. Decide specifically where you want to go, what you want to achieve, and what level of success or prosperity you want to enjoy.
2. Choose the level of productivity you'll have to achieve in order for you to be so rewarded.
3. Decide to what extent you'll have to work through other people to achieve this level of productivity.
4. Develop the skills, knowledge, and abilities you'll need in order to get what you need done through people.

Are you willing to sit down and respond to these four actions? Are you willing to start, realizing that it may take time to come up with specific, measurable strategies. Undoubtedly, you'll need to ask the counsel of successful people who can share their experiences with you. You'll have to study, read, and learn about leadership traits and skills. And, of course, search for and discover that "something else" that I've mentioned earlier.

Leadership Skills or Traits

Let's take a moment to think about some specific leadership/ coaching skills or traits. The following is a list of characteristics I have noticed in effective leaders. Take a look, then read the description of each.

1. *Vision*
2. *Charisma*
3. *Character*

 4. *Responsibility*

 5. *Planning*

 6. *Social Skills*

 7. *Achievement Drive*

 8. *Emotional Stability*

 9. *Tolerance for Ambiguity*

10. *Decisiveness*

11. *Delegation*

12. *Positive Outlook*

Now let's explore each of these in more detail.

Vision

Vision is having a clear picture of where you're going. It's not only having a clear goal, but it's also having a strong commitment to reaching it. This commitment is expressed in your actions and confidence level. You have a deep belief that your objectives are possible and that you'll find a way to achieve them. You're constantly designing, revising, and carrying out your plans of action.

When your vision or mission is energized by strong purpose (and is congruent with your values and beliefs), you become strong, powerful, and effective.

Emerson once wrote, "The world makes way for the man who knows where he's going." It's still true today. The world *does* make way for the person who knows where he or she is going.

Try an experiment while walking down a crowded sidewalk. Walk for a couple blocks specifically attempting to avoid colliding with people. As they walk toward you, watch where they seem to want to go and then move out of their way.

Do this and you'll soon discover that you're jumping around in every direction.

But then set your sights dead ahead, looking at a specific point instead of looking at people. Walk resolutely in that direction, looking beyond the people, and you'll discover that everyone steps aside as you walk through the crowd. It's a very simple example of the truth: "The world makes way for the person who knows where she or he is going!"

People seem to have a sixth sense about whether or not we know where we're going. When they sense that we do, they'll line up behind us. They'll step aside for us. They are unconsciously drawn to us when we are passionately pulled toward productive objectives and causes. People like crusaders—individuals who exhibit the flame of passion and conviction as they march toward exciting causes and purposes.

Charisma

Charisma is a winsome quality that causes people to like us or respect us, and want to emulate us. Difficult to describe, it is a deep attitude about who we are, what we're about, and where we're going. It begins as high self-esteem that's then passionately directed toward goals and objectives.

It's energy. It springs from trusting the rightness of your course and beliefs; from a sense of destiny, having discovered and claimed the gifts with which you've been uniquely endowed.

Charisma always appears natural. Never feigned or contrived but as easy as the flow of nature. It has an obvious harmony and congruence. Emerson wrote so eloquently in his essay on "Friendship," "A man who stands united with his thought conceives magnificently of himself. He is conscious of a universal success. . . ."

This dynamic energy not only gives you high levels of power and energy, but it also causes you to have a natural high expectation of others. You have a natural assertiveness and you trust implicitly others' commitment to results.

Charisma isn't flashiness or eloquence although it can appear as such. It also can be demonstrated by quietness and humility—quiet strength elicits trust and confidence.

Charisma is the spirit of a person radiating hope, concern, confidence, love, excitement, or high expectations of others.

Charisma alone can be hollow or even destructive when not tempered with wisdom and strong values. The con man or sociopath possesses charisma, but when he or she relies too heavily on it, it always brings the deceiver destruction. Such people are almost always found out, and their lack of integrity exposes them.

Charisma causes people to want to be like you, have what you have, or do what you do. Possessors attract others in a silent, compelling way. At the root of their attraction is the internal belief that they have clear vision and goals along with the confidence that they'll accomplish those goals.

Character

Character is the sum of your ideals, values, experience, knowledge, and wisdom. It goes to the centralmost part of you—the "I Am" dimension. Nothing more adequately describes who I am than my character.

It is the composite of my morality, values, and ethics. The strength of my character determines how consistent my values and beliefs will be. Will I compromise? Will I remain true to my values and sense of right and wrong when it would be easier, more beneficial, and more expedient to cut corners and compromise?

Character is doing the right thing because it's the right thing to do. It's telling the truth when lying would be more popular or rewarding. Character allows us to resist pressure from others who might ask us to compromise our integrity in order to gain benefits for themselves.

Few things are communicated more powerfully, though silently, than a person who'll remain steadfast to his or her convictions. Emerson said it like this, "We pass for what we are.

Character teaches above our wills. Men imagine that they communicate their virtue or vice only by overt actions, and do not see that virtue or vice emit a breath every moment."

"Character evermore publishes itself," he also wrote. And in his essay on "Character," he wrote, "Character is nature in its highest form."

People trust leaders whose character embodies integrity, honesty, and straightforwardness. People honor people who live and deal with others in a congruent manner. It's communicated; no one has to publicize it.

People also soon find out about those who would shade the truth and cut ethical corners. And the people who compromise truth and strong values find that their gains are eventually offset by the loss of respect of others.

Responsibility

Responsibility is the willingness to take initiative and accept full accountability for the outcome.

One of the classics of the late 1800s was a booklet by Elbert Hubbard titled *A Message for Garcia*. The story was about a general who gave a letter to a man with the orders, "Take this letter to a man named Garcia who is fighting a battle somewhere in the hills of Cuba."

The man took the letter, saluted, turned to go to Cuba to find Garcia, fighting a war somewhere in the hills. He did not ask, "Where in Cuba is Garcia?" He did not ask, "How will I know when I find him?" He did not ask "What is in the letter?" He did not ask any questions; he simply took the letter, said, "Yes, sir," saluted, and turned to go to Cuba and find a man named Garcia.

Elbert Hubbard's little classic was read by millions and became a runaway best-seller.

His point was simple. Initiative! Assuming responsibility to figure out how to get something done.

Organizations everywhere are looking for people who will

"take the message to Garcia." Who will say "Yes, sir," and use their intelligence and initiative to figure out a way to accomplish their mission. Admittedly, there aren't many of these people—certainly not enough. And, believe me, these people are highly sought after and extremely well paid.

Another crucial characteristic is the willingness to do something without being told. To go beyond what is acceptable and even commendable to what is exceptional.

Planning

Planning is the ability to lay out clear plans and organize people and resources to reach them. Planning occurs after goal clarity is fixed and specific objectives are well-defined. It's simply the question, "Here are our goals or objectives, now how do we get there?"

Sometimes our plans are obvious. Other times we must search for steps to our goals. Our strategy is very often in a state of evolution, with frequent adjustments along the way.

Some people have natural planning skills; others don't. We must spend time learning them. Some people overplan and underexecute; others do the opposite. Some people say, "Ready, fire, aim!" Others say, "Ready, ready, ready . . ." Others, "Ready, aim, aim, aim . . ." Still others say "Gun, I don't see no gun!"

There are those who spend their lives planning but never complete anything because taking action would mean risking failure. Others spend their lives blindly jumping from one move to another, never realizing that often an ounce of planning is worth a pound of action.

Effective leaders balance planning and execution. They know how and why to plan. They know how and when to take action.

Social Skills

We need social skills to deal with people. Social skills are our ability to listen, to understand, and to respond smoothly in different situations involving people.

Effective leaders often have highly developed intuition. They sense what people are feeling and thinking. They like people, know how to communicate with them, and are at ease in various social situations.

Socially skilled people recognize that people have different behavior styles; they think differently, make decisions differently, move at different speeds, have different energy levels, have different focuses, and view the world differently. Having social skills means demonstrating the flexibility to adapt to these different styles.

It takes a good bit of maturity to develop strong social skills. First, your self-image needs to be strong enough to allow you to take your focus off yourself and put it on others. Self-focused people can't really listen effectively. Others are poor listeners by nature. When you feel reasonably good about yourself, you can focus on and value others.

There's an even deeper dimension that influences your social skills. It's having a warm regard for others. Call it a genuine interest or caring spirit that subconsciously manifests itself and acts as a magnet to attract others to you. This power isn't a conscious, logical, measurable thing. It's a value within you that sends out positive, congruent thoughts that others find pleasant, stimulating, and attractive.

Achievement Drive

Achievement drive is the ability to release strong commitment, energy, and persistence toward the attainment of goals. Achievement drive is born of desire. It's released from within, rather than poured in from without. It's released when you

have goal clarity and when you internally believe these objectives are reachable. No achievement drive is released if you
don't believe your goals are possible.

Achievement drive is the *need* for achievement. An inner
need that cries out for fulfillment. It could be the need for
recognition, financial security, self-expression, or enjoyment.
Maybe you need to please others, or to win, to compete, prove
to yourself and others that you are adequate, or satisfy insecurities that formed earlier in life.

Much of achievement drive springs from *creative dissatisfaction*—a burning desire to have it better than you've had it.
Poverty or personal insecurities in your formative years often
cause a deep desire for something better to well up inside you.

There's a certain unrest within high achievement drive people that keeps them from resting on their laurels. It pushes,
prods, and motivates. This can be a blessing or a curse—the
drive can be creative or, in the extreme, neurotic.

High achievers aren't usually normal people. Not content to
float through life, they challenge circumstances; they blaze new
trails. They must explore the other side of the mountain. They
want to find ways to do it better.

They're highly motivated to take action. They may be motivated by money or what money will buy, by recognition or
the benefits of recognition, by power or prestige, by security
or the acceptance of others.

This motivation can be constructive or destructive. It largely
depends on their underlying values. If they have strong, positive values, their achievement drive will be constructive. For
people with weak values, their achievement drive can be destructive—it can lead them to do things that are illegal, im-
moral, or unethical.

Almost every new advance or discovery in life comes because
of the need for achievement in individuals. Where high
achievement drive exists—individually, corporately, or country-
wide—productivity and prosperity are high.

Strong leaders exhibit high achievement drive and model it

for their people. That climate helps others develop it in their own lives.

Emotional Stability

Emotional stability is balance, poise, and the ability to maintain an even emotional level through ups and downs.

In his excellent best-seller, *Emotional Intelligence*, Daniel Goleman differentiates emotional intelligence (EQ) from intellectual intelligence (IQ). He begins by writing that people with high IQ usually work for people who have high EQ.

Emotional intelligence is knowing how to apply our intellectual intelligence. It's being able to maintain emotional balance despite the slings and arrows that life throws at you. Emotional intelligence is wisdom—the gift of discernment.

Emotional stability begins with how you feel about who you are. If you like yourself and feel fairly adequate, then you'll project confidence in your responses and reactions. It's the ability to look at life over the long haul—knowing there will be ups and downs and believing that you can use both as learning experiences. It's also the belief that you need both highs and lows to make you stronger in order to prepare for what you're meant to become.

As your emotional stability grows, you tend not to have mood swings, rather your responses tend to level out. You meet both good and not-so-good experiences head-on and react in a stable, consistent manner whether you get rewarded or banged up.

Emotional stability is, in a nutshell, *maturity*.

Tolerance for Ambiguity

A cousin of Emotional Stability, Tolerance for Ambiguity is the ability to handle stress, disappointment, roadblocks, and frustrating experiences while maintaining progress, your goals clearly in sight.

High achievers usually have the ability to juggle lots of balls in the air while maintaining their focus, purpose, and self-control. In fact, if they don't have lots of balls in the air, they pitch a few more into the juggling act.

Another unique trait of effective leaders is the ability to view situations in the micro and macro—to see the big picture and how the details fit into it. This isn't a natural characteristic but one that probably has been developed. There are, of course, highly effective leaders who see only the big picture and surround themselves with people who watch the details. Some people—perfectionists—tend to focus on the details while missing the big picture.

Leaders are also calculated risk-takers—not oil-field wild-catters who risk everything on the drilling of a well, but takers of logical, prudent risks.

Decisiveness

Decisiveness is the ability to assess situations, analyze alternatives, and move toward goal solutions. Decisiveness often results from good instincts and the willingness to run risks. It develops as you learn to trust your judgments and inclinations.

Effective decision makers get all the facts and then take action. Often they must make decisions without all the facts. It's here that intuition and "gut feel" come in.

Napoleon Hill, author of the self-help classic *Think and Grow Rich*, studied the five hundred most financially successful people of his day. He wrote that each one had the common ability, after learning the known facts, to reach quick decisions, stick to them, and slowly change them if and when necessary.

It's here that the strength of a person's commitment to action can actually transform an incorrect decision into a correct one. It is often this commitment that influences less strong people to give way to your strength of purpose.

Decisiveness is an essential component of effective leadership. People do not follow weak or wobbly decision makers.

Delegation

Delegation is the ability to assign projects to competent people and to review and inspect their performance regularly.

Many people are promoted to leadership positions because of their ability to get things done by themselves. They can often sell more or accomplish more than other people, so they're elevated to management roles. Often they make poor managers because they can't delegate or achieve through others. So, they hit their heads on the low ceiling of leadership or they keep trying to do everything themselves, leading to stress, frustration, or even chaos. The inability to delegate, for Doer-type people, often becomes a stumbling block. It takes real effort and demands that new habits be formed.

Effective delegation first demands that you have competent people to assign work to; then it demands you trust them to do the job. Finally, it involves inspecting the work you've delegated.

It's only by delegation that you can really multiply yourself and get more done through people—which, as I've said before, will determine the level of your rewards.

Positive Outlook

A positive outlook is an internal belief that good will prevail and goals will be reached. It's "Possibility Thinking," to borrow a phrase from Dr. Robert Schuller.

You have your own view of your possibilities. Within your emotional and creative self, you hold a powerful belief about what's possible for you to achieve, and what's not possible. Whatever internal belief is, all your actions, feelings, behavior, and abilities are consistent with it.

A positive outlook is revealed by attitudes of "what can go

right" not "what can go wrong." It's the subconscious belief in successful outcomes. It's believing that anything is possible and that with good plans and diligent, persistent effort goals can and will be reached. It's prepared optimism, not pie-in-the-sky fantasy. It's believing that the best will happen with diligent effort.

Leadership Skills Survey

At the end of this chapter is a Personal Leadership Survey that you can photocopy and score yourself. Hand it out to a few people who know you to score. Tell them not to put their names on the sheets so you won't know who did each one. You'll get more accurate assessments this way.

Summing Up

Organizations everywhere are searching for people to whom they can pay lots of money for taking responsibility and getting more done through people.

Getting more done through people is how you leverage yourself. The more you get done through the most people, the more you're paid—either in money, recognition, respect, security, or self-fulfillment.

Knowing this you may want to ask yourself these three questions.

1. "How much do I want to earn or achieve?"
2. "Okay, if this is how much I want to earn or achieve, then what level of results will I have to take responsibility for making happen in order to earn this much?"
3. "Well, now, am I willing to take action and do this?"

I outlined twelve leadership traits and briefly defined each one. Reread these several times and then score yourself on the following Leadership Skills Survey. Photocopy it and have several people with whom you work evaluate you. Be sure and ask them *not* to identify themselves so you'll get a more honest score.

Earlier I emphasized that the sum of leadership skills will not necessarily make you a leader—that it takes the mix of a special ingredient, a "something else." I won't attempt to tell you what that "something else" is. You must discover it for yourself, but I will drop hints throughout this book. If you're truly looking, you will find it.

You will discover it within yourself—not externally, but intrinsically. That's my first clue.

Leadership Skills Survey

Vision	Never descriptive	Somewhat descriptive	Always descriptive
I have a clear picture of where I want to go.		1 2 3 4 5 6 7 8 9 10	
I am strongly motivated by a sense of purpose or mission.		1 2 3 4 5 6 7 8 9 10	
My values are congruent with our organization's core values.		1 2 3 4 5 6 7 8 9 10	
I stay focused on objectives despite problems or distractions.		1 2 3 4 5 6 7 8 9 10	

TOTAL _____

Charisma

I have a strong sense of purpose that attracts others to me.	1 2 3 4 5 6 7 8 9 10
I have the ability to excite people and help them feel better about themselves when they're around me.	1 2 3 4 5 6 7 8 9 10
People tell me that I have an energy level that they find attracting.	1 2 3 4 5 6 7 8 9 10
Others see qualities in me that they'd like to possess.	1 2 3 4 5 6 7 8 9 10

TOTAL _____

Character

I diligently carry through on commitments I make.	1 2 3 4 5 6 7 8 9 10
I have strong, positive values that guide my actions.	1 2 3 4 5 6 7 8 9 10

	Never descriptive	Somewhat descriptive	Always descriptive

I always do the right thing rather than the expedient thing.

    1 2 3 4 5 6 7 8 9 10

People who know me know that I'll always be honest and truthful with them.

    1 2 3 4 5 6 7 8 9 10

TOTAL _____

Responsibility

I'm someone others turn to when they want something done.

    1 2 3 4 5 6 7 8 9 10

I'm extremely conscientious and diligent in getting things done.

    1 2 3 4 5 6 7 8 9 10

When I say, "I'll do it," you can depend on me.

    1 2 3 4 5 6 7 8 9 10

I have a strong sense of accountability.

    1 2 3 4 5 6 7 8 9 10

TOTAL _____

Planning

I'm able to lay out clear plans of how to get things done.

    1 2 3 4 5 6 7 8 9 10

I achieve a good balance between planning and execution.

    1 2 3 4 5 6 7 8 9 10

I am very effective in working with others in planning activities.

    1 2 3 4 5 6 7 8 9 10

I have excellent analytical skills in deciding what needs to be done to achieve goals.

    1 2 3 4 5 6 7 8 9 10

TOTAL _____

Social Skills

	Never descriptive	Somewhat descriptive	Always descriptive

I adjust well to different types of people and situations.

1 2 3 4 5 6 7 8 9 10

I listen well and am sensitive to people's ideas and needs.

1 2 3 4 5 6 7 8 9 10

I am especially effective at calming people in stressful situations.

1 2 3 4 5 6 7 8 9 10

I am highly intuitive—able to pick up on people's unspoken meanings.

1 2 3 4 5 6 7 8 9 10

TOTAL _____

Achievement Drive

I demonstrate high drive and desire for goals.

1 2 3 4 5 6 7 8 9 10

I am self-motivated and committed to high achievement.

1 2 3 4 5 6 7 8 9 10

I exert a high enough level of energy needed to reach goals.

1 2 3 4 5 6 7 8 9 10

I inspire those around me to release more of their own drive, desire, and motivation.

1 2 3 4 5 6 7 8 9 10

TOTAL _____

Emotional Stability

I maintain a fairly level emotional response during ups and downs.

1 2 3 4 5 6 7 8 9 10

I always keep my composure even when others are losing theirs.

1 2 3 4 5 6 7 8 9 10

	Never descriptive	Somewhat descriptive	Always descriptive

I am quite comfortable with who
I am.

1 2 3 4 5 6 7 8 9 10

I am able to discuss negative
issues without becoming stinging
or hurtful.

1 2 3 4 5 6 7 8 9 10

TOTAL _____

Tolerance for Ambiguity

I have an amazing ability to
juggle lots of balls in the air and
still focus on objectives.

1 2 3 4 5 6 7 8 9 10

I'm very adaptable and flexible in
making it through stressful
situations.

1 2 3 4 5 6 7 8 9 10

I work well with a wide diversity
of people.

1 2 3 4 5 6 7 8 9 10

I'm able to work through clutter
and get to the real issues.

1 2 3 4 5 6 7 8 9 10

TOTAL _____

Decisiveness

I'm able to get at important facts,
analyze them, and come to a
decision.

1 2 3 4 5 6 7 8 9 10

My decisions are usually
influenced by a strong sense of
right and wrong.

1 2 3 4 5 6 7 8 9 10

I make decisions in the best
interest of our organization.

1 2 3 4 5 6 7 8 9 10

Once a decision is made, I stick
with it.

1 2 3 4 5 6 7 8 9 10

TOTAL _____

Delegation

	Never descriptive	Somewhat descriptive	Always descriptive

I effectively assign jobs and projects to people that fit their unique abilities.

1 2 3 4 5 6 7 8 9 10

I communicate expectations very clearly.

1 2 3 4 5 6 7 8 9 10

I'm excellent at getting things done through people.

1 2 3 4 5 6 7 8 9 10

I follow up well and inspect people's performance.

1 2 3 4 5 6 7 8 9 10

TOTAL _____

Positive Outlook

I have a strong sense of optimism that's tempered with reality.

1 2 3 4 5 6 7 8 9 10

My "can do" attitude inspires all the people around me.

1 2 3 4 5 6 7 8 9 10

I seem to see a "silver lining" in every cloud.

1 2 3 4 5 6 7 8 9 10

I have a deep, underlying belief that things will turn out right despite setbacks and frustrations.

1 2 3 4 5 6 7 8 9 10

TOTAL _____

Leadership Skills Graph

	Vision	Charisma	Character	Responsibility	Planning	Social Skills	Achievement Drive	Emotional Stability	Tolerance for Ambiguity	Decisiveness	Delegation	Positive Outlook
10												
9												
8												
7												
6												
5												
4												
3												
2												
1												

Please plot your scores on the above graph and connect your dots.

How to Gain the Most from This Chapter

Follow these suggestions and you'll gain the most from this chapter.

1. Focus on it for one week.
2. Read it through and then go back and reread it several times during the week—making notes and underlining.
3. Ask yourself.
   a. "What level of success, achievement, and prosperity do I want to enjoy?"
   b. "What level of productivity will I need to make happen in order to enjoy the above level?"
   c. "To what extent will I have to work through others in order to achieve this level?"
   d. "What skills, knowledge, or abilities will I need in order to reach it?"
4. Look over the twelve characteristics of leadership and then score yourself on the assessment at the end of the chapter.
5. Ask yourself this question several times each day: "How can I cause more productivity to come from more people?"
6. Write down the ideas you think of for question #5 and make a commitment to practice one or two of the best ones.

People will just naturally get more done when you regularly and systematically coach them into new levels of self-discovery and personal effectiveness!

3. People Rise to Their Belief of Your Belief in Them.

In teaching, it is the method and not the content that is the message . . . the drawing out, not the pumping in.

—ASHLEY MONTAGU

People will rise to meet the level of your expectations of them. Set thoroughbred expectations for people, and they'll perform nearer that level. Set plow horse expectations, and they'll perform accordingly.

In this chapter I'll share with you a powerful Coaching and Counseling Model that when consistently and sincerely implemented will cause significant improvement in your people.

That's a promise!

You hold me to it, okay?

"But," you challenge, "you can't create a racehorse out of a plow horse!" I agree. I'm saying you can help your people reach their own individual potential through effective coaching. You can help them become more of what they're capable of becoming.

If your people are normal, 80 percent of them are now performing well under their possibilities. Do you agree? The other

20 percent are highly motivated and probably performing on a very satisfactory level. When we conduct our training courses for organizations, we find that these top 20 percent are often the most eager to learn—primarily because they have higher achievement drives. Ironically, they usually gain the most from our training. And since they're already performing on a high level, percentage gains show significant bottom-line improvements.

The average manager can cause significant productivity gains with positive, effective coaching; by building people; by taking people and helping them develop their undiscovered skills, talents, and abilities. All of us need coaches. Most people will not work, learn, and extend themselves, by themselves, to the extent they will with the help of a coach who sets high expectations for them.

A friend of mine, Art Zorka, a magician and speaker in Atlanta, tells an incredible story that illustrates this point.

One day he was in the New Orleans airport waiting for a flight back to Atlanta. Hearing a big noise from people he looked and saw Muhammad Ali walking toward him amid throngs of reporters and people. Ali walked up to where Art was standing, stopped, looked at Art, and said, "Put 'em up champ!"

Not knowing what to do, Art, put up his fists like a fighter. This must have looked pretty funny because Art is just above five feet tall.

Ali laughed and said, "No, no," and then reached over and turned Art's palms up. He then set a briefcase in his hands and opened it, revealing all sorts of magic "things."

"Do you do magic?" Art asked, surprised.

"Yeah."

"I do magic, too," Art responded.

"Yeah, I know," Ali said.

"How'd you know?"

"Because I'm the greatest! I know everything!" Ali grinned. Then he pointed to Art's case on the floor that had printed on it, "Magic is a vanishing Art."

Ali arranged for Art to sit by him on the airplane, and they did magic stuff all the way to Atlanta. Art told me that he couldn't believe that Ali's huge hands were so agile and skilled.

Before reaching Atlanta, Art asked him, "Champ, I speak to audiences all the time. Would you tell me what the greatest lesson you've learned from life is, so I can share it with people?"

Ali thought a moment, and then said, "It was February 25, 1964, in Miami. I was Cassius Clay fighting Sonny Liston for the heavyweight title. He was the strongest man I'd ever fought. Every time I hit him, it hurt me worse than it did him. I gave him everything I had.

"When the sixth round ended, I was completely spent. I couldn't even raise my arms. I couldn't even stand up to go back into the ring. 'I'm goin' home!' I told Angelo Dundee. 'I'm not going back in there!' "

"Hearing this," Ali explained, "Angelo Dundee pushed his upper body into the ring and screamed at him to get ready to go in, only to get a refusal." "I can't do it. I'm goin' home!" Then the bell rang. Dundee pushed at Ali and screamed, "Get in there and don't come out until you are the Heavyweight Champion of the World!"

Because of Dundee's screams, Ali struggled to his feet. The rest is history. Sonny Liston didn't answer the bell, and Ali became the champion.

Hearing this, Art anticipated that Ali's lesson was "Keep on keeping on. Make one last effort. Get up every time you're knocked down." But that wasn't it. Making his point, Ali said, "You tell your audiences that the greatest lesson I've learned is to have someone pushin' you and makin' you do things you don't think you can do! That's the greatest lesson I've learned. You tell your audiences that!"

No successful coach ever says to his or her players, "Okay, gang, you go out and learn whatever you can and practice whatever you want to, and be sure and show up for game day." No coach would ever be so naive as to think that players would push themselves enough to develop the level of conditioning and skills that it takes to win. The legendary Vince Lombardi once said, "You've got to make professional athletes do what they don't want to do, and didn't enjoy doing, but are glad they did!"

Most People Set Standards That Are Well Within Their Capabilities

Most people *do* set lower standards than they're capable of achieving—it's human nature. As a manager, you already know this. This wisdom was well stated by the great German writer and statesman Johann W. von Goethe when he said, "Treat people as if they were what they ought to be and you help them to become what they are capable of being."

The great thinker Ashley Montagu put it like this, "By virtue of being born to humanity, every human being has a right to the development and fulfillment of his potential as a human being." And it was the father of modern psychology, Harvard professor and prolific author William James, who wrote the following, "Compared with what we ought to be, we are only half-awake. We are making use of only a small part of our physical and mental resources. Stating the thing broadly, the human individual thus lives far within his limits. He possesses power of various sorts which he habitually fails to use."

People do live and think well below their potential. We see this all the time in our course participants. But, you know what? Across the board, in numerous organizations, people are producing almost *exactly* what managers or leaders *expect* them to produce.

People fall into ruts and habits. They gravitate to levels of productivity that they think are acceptable by managers. After a very short time, these levels become fixed beliefs about what they should be producing. They become their unconscious "areas of the possible." Then whatever these mental paradigms or beliefs are get carried out in their work. It makes no difference what a person does—selling, customer service, loading trucks, data entry, manufacturing widgets—their unconscious beliefs about "what's possible for me to produce" become self-fulfilling. People's output becomes consistent with what they internally "see" themselves producing.

One of our clients was the Chevrolet Motor Division. I wrote their *Integrity Selling*® program installed in about nine hundred larger dealerships. Another project was developing a unique customer-satisfaction process. In doing this, I learned about their customer-concerns department. As I recall, there were around five hundred sharp, bright young people on telephones in a center taking incoming calls. For the first three months on the job, not knowing what the norm was, new people averaged close to forty-eight calls a day. They were required to take at least twenty-five calls per day. And strangely enough, after six months, their calls dropped from forty-eight to twenty-five per day.

Unconsciously, over time, they gravitated to the levels of the minimally acceptable manager expectations. Undoubtedly, there were other factors that influenced this pattern, but the fact is that the number of calls dropped precipitously.

The truth is that many managers communicate what level of production is acceptable and their people unconsciously adjust their work accordingly. After adjusting to this "norm," they continue on that level. Then managers' paradigms about what they expect from each person become fixed, which in turn reinforces their people's productivity and so on. Each reinforces the other.

People Produce More When Managers Regularly Coach and Counsel Them

Regularly scheduled coaching and counseling sessions will help improve the performance of almost anyone. In a moment, I'll share a highly effective coaching and counseling process with you. But first, let me explain a couple of things.

This coaching session should be in a completely private setting where no interruptions or distractions are permitted. Communicate the message to the person you're coaching that nothing is more important than this session. The session can be done in fifteen minutes. You'll really have to discipline yourself and carefully follow the process or you'll take longer. It's most effective when you succinctly deal with each of the steps.

Here's the coaching process.

Coaching and Counseling Process

1. *Ask* about their goals or objectives.
   a. Ask, "What specific goals or objectives are you working on, and where are you in respect to them?"
   b. Ask, "What constraints are keeping you from reaching these goals?"
   c. Ask, "What skills, activities, or behaviors will help you move through these constraints or reach these goals?"

2. *Listen* without distractions or interruptions.
   a. Listen to people's words, tone of voice, and body language.
   b. Guide and question them and help them discover their own answers.
   c. Believe that their answers are within them, waiting to be discovered.

3. *Coach* knowledge, skills, or actions as needed.
   a. Confront constraints, problem issues, or needed areas of improvement.
   b. Suggest one action that will help them remove a constraint or move toward a goal.
   c. Keep the responsibility on their shoulders, not yours.

4. *Praise* specific behaviors.
   a. Point out specific talents, skills, attitudes, knowledge, or abilities they have that will help them reach goals.
   b. Express your belief that they will do whatever it takes to be successful.

c. Explain potential you see in them that they don't see in themselves.
5. *Challenge* them to become their best.
   a. Ask them to commit to specific goals, results, and time frames.
   b. Explain that you will follow-up and hold them accountable.
   c. Thank them and remind them how important they are to your organization.

To help remember these five steps, use this memory stacking method. Visualize:

1. A huge pair of red wax lips that *ask* questions.
2. Placed to the right of them is a massive pink plastic ear with a mole on it that *listens*.
3. Standing with one foot on the huge red wax lips that *ask* questions, and the other on the massive pink plastic ear with a mole on it that *listens*, is a confident, enthusiastic *coach*.
4. In the coach's right hand is a giant blue letter "P" that reminds him or her to *praise* the players.
5. In the coach's left hand is a giant red letter "C" that reminds him or her to *challenge* the players.

So . . . *ask, listen, coach, praise, challenge*!

Now, let me talk about this process for a moment.

First, let me emphasize that this *isn't a performance review*. You should make that very clear to your people before you conduct each session—at least until they experience the positiveness of it. Then they'll look forward to each coaching session because they will view it as a positive experience.

In addition, I need to tell you that you'll need to do a half dozen of these sessions before they'll feel comfortable to you. I recommend that you copy the model on a card and use it as a guide when you conduct the coaching session. Just lay it on your desk or table and follow each point. This will make you look organized. It will give you a clear, simple track to follow. It will keep you from talking too much yourself—which diminishes the effect of the session.

Let's think of several suggestions that can add to the effectiveness of your coaching.

1. *Be sincere.* Before the session, clearly identify your purpose—to build people and help them discover more of the potential that you see in them.

2. *Treat people as unique individuals.* Measure them against themselves, not others.

3. *Accept people as they are.* You can't change the basic emotional set of people. Accept their weaknesses and build on their strengths. Everyone has strengths and weaknesses. You'll always strengthen whichever you focus on. Don't just try to make people eliminate their weaknesses. Let them tell you what areas they want to improve in. This allows them to take ownership of constraints without ego damage. You can usually cause all the productivity increases you want by focusing on people's strengths and helping them build those.

4. *Challenge people to keep goals fairly short range.* Suggest they focus on 5 to 10 percent increases. This will give them a target that they can reach in a fairly short period. When they reach it, get them to set another 5 or 10 percent goal. Short-range goals give us frequent successes and gratification.

5. *Practice discovery learning.* Not all managers know much about this, but great leaders do. Discovery learning is asking people questions that cause them to discover their own answers, rather than your telling them the answers. This is built on sound learning dynamics. People are more apt to learn, remember, and practice what they discover for themselves than what you tell them.

6. *Make notes.* Write down their goals and other important points that you'll want to refer to during your next coaching session preparation.

Listen More Than You Talk

Your coaching objective is to help people learn and improve their performance. They rarely do this just by hearing you tell them what to do. If this worked, you'd have few problems with employee productivity because all you'd have to do is tell them what to do and how to do it, and they'd then do their jobs perfectly. No problem. Life would be pretty simple, wouldn't it?

Mark Van Doren put it aptly when he wrote, "The art of teaching is the art of consistent discovery." Or, as an old Chinese proverb goes, "I hear and I forget. I see and I remember. I do and I understand."

Steps 1 and 2 (ask about goals and objectives and listen without distraction or interruptions) will take up three-fourths of your session time. In these steps you're asking appropriate questions and listening—spending 20 percent of the time asking questions and 80 percent of the time listening.

Now, what I know is that the more of a Doer-type personality you have, the more difficult it'll be for you to ask questions that cause people to think and discover. It's easier to tell people what you want them to know than to be quiet and listen. So you'll have to convince yourself of the value of this process, and adjust your natural behaviors accordingly.

Questions You Can Ask People During Your Coaching Sessions

Here are several questions you can ask during your coaching sessions. Notice that most of these questions contain the words *who, what, where, why, when, how*. They call for responses, not just "yes" or "no" answers.

1. "How did our last coaching session benefit you?"

2. "What specific work-related goals are you working on?"

3. "How do you measure what you do?"

4. "How are you progressing toward these goals?"

5. "Where are you now in relation to where you have to go?"

6. "How realistic do you feel your goals are now?"

7. "What are some specific activities that you're doing to reach your goals?"

8. "How is your own belief in what's possible for you to be achieving changing?"

9. "What skills will it take to reach your goals?"

10. "What new work habits will it take to reach your goals?"

11. "What new knowledge do you need in order to reach your goals?"

12. "What time-management skills are you working on?"

13. "What factors, outside the job, are influencing your work quality or productivity?"

14. "How would the people who work around you describe your skill level?"

15. "What would the people who work around you tell me that your major strengths are?"

16. "What personal trait are you currently focusing on building?"

17. "What are some thoughts you have about how we can increase our overall productivity?"

18. "What are some ways that you think we can increase our team effectiveness?"

19. "How can I help you do your job better?"

20. "What specific actions can I take to support you in achieving your goals?"

How to Prepare for a Coaching Session

Take a few minutes and prepare for each coaching session by doing the following.

1. Review previous coaching sessions. Get a feel for where the people are, what their strengths are, and in what areas you want them to improve.
2. Write down a few questions (using the previous list as a guide) that will cause the people to think and discover what you want them to learn.
3. Visualize them performing on the level you want them on.

Your Beliefs in Them Will Strongly Influence Them

When your coaching sessions are positive and building and when you sell people on your belief in their ability, you'll impact them much more strongly.

I firmly believe that the following three factors strongly influence people's productivity.

1. To the degree that *you* sincerely believe that they can achieve higher performance.
2. To the degree that they believe that *you* believe that.
3. To the degree that there is trust, mutual respect, and rapport between *you* and them.

Stop and spend some time mulling over what I've just said. When these three factors are present, your people will develop faster and increase their productivity.

New Role of a Manager

What I've presented to you in this chapter, as well as this whole book, may place you as a manager or supervisor in a different role than you've traditionally been cast. This role shift takes you from a person who manages processes, budgets, quotas, activities, or bottom lines to one who builds people.

In order to enjoy larger rewards yourself, you must get more done through people. To win in the years ahead, you must increase individual productivity, and to do that you'll have to learn to build your people. You must be as skilled in building people as you are at managing processes. In many cases this involves a whole new level of knowledge and skills. Admittedly, this is a different view of managing.

Traits of a Good Leader, Coach, or Counselor

Let me mention some traits and attitudes that are important for effective coaching. Let's take a moment and define your role:

1. To do a lot of listening and get feedback from people on their job performance or goal achievement.
2. To ask questions that get people discovering their abilities, needs, and improvement areas.
3. To see more strengths in them than they see in themselves.
4. To empower them by believing in and having confidence in them.
5. To get commitments from them for specific activities and results.
6. To lead by example.
7. To demonstrate a positive attitude at all times—about your job, the organization, and senior management.

8. To demonstrate consistency in your personal behavior and your relations with people.

9. To understand that different people have different needs.

10. To maintain optimism and confidence in the direction of your organization.

Your Role Is Not:

1. To dominate the conversation and tell people what they're not doing well or should be doing better.

2. To focus more on their weaknesses than on their strengths.

3. To criticize or put down.

4. To withhold praise and encouragement.

5. To preach instead of lead.

6. To criticize your organization or your management.

7. To show favoritism.

8. To say one thing and do another.

9. To not walk your talk.

10. To be cynical and suspicious.

Summing Up

I preceded this chapter by quoting Ashley Montagu's powerful truth:

> In teaching it is the method and not the content that is the message ... the drawing out, not the pumping in.

Teaching/coaching is like that. I call it Discovery Learning—people are more apt to learn, internalize, and practice what they discover for themselves than what you tell them.

Not all managers know this. Most leaders do.

I've emphasized that people will often rise to your level of expectations. People tend to produce what's expected. This explains a lot of both high and low performance. It seems to me that this is a Law of Limited Performance.

> People soon discover the level of performance that their managers will settle for and gravitate to that level. Managers then assume that's all that people are capable of achieving, so they accept it as fact and quit challenging their people to get better. So, each reinforces what the other believes.

I gave you a Coaching and Counseling model that incorporates all the steps you need to build your people's performance. All you have to add is sincerity, belief in the person's potential, and, of course, application.

Remember, you'll need to do it to the letter at least six times before it'll feel comfortable. Remember, too, that it *isn't* a performance appraisal. Let your people know that.

Let me emphasize what I said about your own attitudes influencing your coaching success. I mentioned three factors that powerfully influence people's productivity:

1. Your sincere belief that they can achieve higher performance.

2. Their belief that *you* believe that.

3. The degree of trust, mutual respect, and rapport between *you* and them.

Yes, of all the factors that influence your people's productivity, your own expectations of and belief in them certainly rank near the top of the list.

How to Gain the Most from This Chapter

Here are some suggestions that will help you gain the most from this chapter.

1. Read it through to get an overall view of what's covered.
2. Go back through, underline important points, and make action notes in the margins.
3. Transfer the Coaching and Counseling Model onto a card, sheet of paper, or into your organizer or computer.
4. Set up at least six coaching sessions and follow the model exactly. Keep notes from your meetings for later reference. Keep most of your sessions under fifteen minutes.
5. Ask yourself the following questions:
   a. "How much growth potential does each of my people have?"
   b. "If my own expectations of people are self-fulfilling prophecies, then how can I begin to view each person in a more positive way?"
   c. "What do I need to do to move from just being a manager to being a leader?"

My best to you. I expect you to have a breakthrough week!

People often get stuck, stalled, burned out, and you can't help them until you understand what's pressing their buttons and screaming for attention in their lives!

4. When You Accept People as They Are, They Immediately Want to Get Better.

The most immutable barrier in nature is between one man's thoughts and another's.

—WILLIAM JAMES

Since the beginning of time, people have been trying to better understand other people—to understand *who* they are and *why* they *act*, *think*, and *perform* the way they do.

After the fall, I just bet that poor old Adam never understood why he and Eve couldn't go back to the days in the garden before they discovered the need for fig leaves. Or she may have lamented, "Look, now that we're not perfect anymore, why do you have to lie around the house and do nothing but watch football games while I cook, slave, and take care of these kids?"

Or when Cain and Abel each turned sixteen, Adam must have bumped his forehead with the heel of his hand and in exasperation said to Eve, "What's this world coming to? These modern kids expect so much more than we would have if we'd ever been teenagers."

History is full of examples of people not understanding each other. Alexander the Great wept at having no other nations to conquer. How do you understand a mind like that? Hitler couldn't understand why other nations were so intent on slowing down his moves to conquer the world.

Your boss doesn't quite understand your need to go to the Little League game with your children and not to work until midnight preparing a report that he forgot to ask you to work up a week ago. You know or work around oppositional people who see a cloud in every silver lining, and you think to yourself, *I just don't understand this person. Don't they know that their negativity turns people off?*

And so it goes. Our relations get all jammed up because we fail to understand others.

The Need to Be Understood

I'm convinced that one of the strongest needs in human nature is the need to be understood. It's your genuine attempt to understand people without filters or biases that will lay the foundation for effective communication.

Will Rogers has been frequently quoted as saying that he never met a man he didn't like. We've heard this often and pass it off as some famous person saying something that he thought people wanted to hear but didn't really believe himself. It was only after several years of listening to people in my development courses that I understood what he probably meant. From my own experience, I can rephrase Will Rogers's remark to say, "I never met a person that I really got to know that I didn't like!"

I've listened to thousands of people share their lives. I've been able, clinically, to listen to them nonjudgmentally. To accept them as they are—valuable people created in the very image of God. At one point or another, within the weeks of our courses, almost everyone consciously or unconsciously tells of life experiences that explain why they act and think as they do. I've heard people, who at first, kept me at a safe distance emotionally, share traumatic experiences that explained their behavior. From a person who had no apparent ability to feel telling about his training in the Green Berets to kill and dispassionately watch others die; to a person who was suspicious and unapproachable who began to trust the other people and tell of being raped by her brothers as she grew up. It was only when they trusted the group that they could share the pain they'd never been able to reveal before.

Or about the transformation in worker relations that happened when a quiet young man in London who left work early each Friday and incurred the anger of coworkers. Then they found out that each Friday he drove from London to Wales and worked with the Welsh Mountain Rescue Squad that rescued people from accidents. With no fanfare, he'd helped rescue scores of people and had saved a dozen people, personally, by giving them mouth-to-mouth resuscitation. The young man never told them what he did. It was only after someone discovered it that he went from being a difficult person to approach and understand to someone they admired and respected highly.

Simply Understanding People Releases Power

Carl Rogers, the father of modern-day nondirective counseling, has helped many of us discover the power of listening and understanding people. He believes that your greatest power to help people facilitate change in their own lives is to listen nonjudgmentally and give unconditional acceptance to them. In the act of understanding others, we facilitate their growth. We take away barriers and give them freedom to grow.

I have built my whole training philosophy around a statement Rogers once made. He wrote, "When I accept myself as I am, I change. When I accept others as they are, they change!" This is the paradox of change and personal growth. The concept conflicts with our natural minds and ego states. The natural mind seeks to change others by telling them what they're doing wrong and what they need to do to shape themselves up. This almost never works. It usually reinforces their wrong actions (wrong, at least in our opinions). Our natural ego state says to others, "Look I can't accept you as you are, because I don't approve of what you're doing!"

In our courses, we train facilitators to create a noncritical atmosphere and give unconditional acceptance to people. To look at them and see valuable, God-created people. To listen without biases. To listen nonjudgmentally. To look for and focus on their strengths. Many people fight us at first, feeling uncomfortable at receiving unconditional acceptance—not being accustomed to it. Many have suffered abuse, confusion, and rejection to the point that unconsciously they aren't comfortable with real acceptance.

"Wait a minute," you may be saying. "Some people do and say things that I can't accept!" I understand. It's here that we must separate the intrinsic worth of people from their actions.

Joshua Liebman once wrote, "Tolerance is the positive and cordial effort to understand another's beliefs, practices and habits without necessarily sharing or accepting them."

Don't Confuse Accepting People with Having to Accept Their Ideas or Beliefs

I've heard many people state, one way or another, "I can't accept you because I don't agree with you!"

It's here that it's easy to confuse the intrinsic worth of a person with what he or she thinks or believes. For many people, the issue of whether or not they understand and can have meaningful communication with others is wrapped up in whether or not they agree with them. It's like they say, "If I agree with what you think, then I'll accept you; but if I don't agree with you, I won't."

With this mind-set, communication becomes very difficult with many people and impossible with others. Only peripheral levels within people are touched, never moving to the core or essence of a person.

I have friends that think and believe a lot of things that are totally different than the way I think—politically, economically, spiritually, and aesthetically. But we communicate and enjoy each other. We do because we value each other, look past things we disagree on, and focus on things we have in common.

I suspect that you work with people who don't really see life the way you do. If you allow it to, it can block your communication with them. Or you can look past things they think and focus on who they are—valuable God-created individuals who have unique gifts and abilities that you can help them actualize in their work lives! Which, of course, is one of the attributes of leadership.

Another trait of leaders who get more done through people is that they can look past the actual productivity level of people and identify unused strengths. When discovered and actualized, these strengths allow them immediately to increase their output. It's to say to people, "I don't accept where *you* think you should be producing as fact. I see more in you than you see in yourself!"

The Law of Limited Performance

As I've mentioned before, it's easy for people to accept fixed production paradigms as reality. Similarly after observing your people's level, it's natural for you to develop beliefs about them that you accept as reality. Their actions reinforce your beliefs about them, and your beliefs reinforce their continued actions.

In many cases, both of you are wrong. I mentioned a phenomenon in the last chapter and called it the Law of Limited Performance.

The Law of Limited Performance, again, is

People soon discover the level of performance their managers will settle for and gravitate to that level. Managers then assume that's all that people are capable of achieving, so they accept it as fact and quit challenging their people to get better. So each reinforces what the other believes.

Well, okay, so much for identifying the problem. Let's move on to factors that cause your people to get stuck on fixed levels of productivity. We'll also think about how you can understand your people in a more in-depth way and how you can help them move to higher levels of personal growth and productivity.

Progression of Human Needs

In a moment I'll share a model with you that explains basic needs and motivations of your people.

First, let me emphasize that your people's behavior is being caused by internal factors. Different dimensions of their lives powerfully influence their work output or productivity levels.

In many cases you probably have no idea, and will never know fully, about what's happening in their private worlds that's motivating their actions. Here are a few factors that influence each person's productivity.

1. Self-Esteem
2. Relationships
3. Financial situation
4. Support systems
5. Background
6. Health and fitness

Of course, there are others, but these go together and powerfully impact a person's output or productivity on the job.

As you'll quickly discover, most of these are out of your range of influence. Certainly many of these influences are difficult, if not impossible, for you to deal with. But as an effective coach you can listen people into discovering how different life situations are influencing them, and possibly help them discover and deal with the causes. This is what the coaching model I gave you in the last chapter is designed to do.

But first, a disclaimer. Let me plainly state that I'm not trying to make a junior psychologist out of you. In no way am I suggesting that you will be prepared to diagnose people's problems and prescribe cures or courses of action. All I want is to give you a simple model to understand people better. It's really a framework for *listening* and *understanding*. It's often that your listening and understanding enables people to discover their own answers and decide to take action.

My experience is that many low-productivity problems can be addressed simply by *listening, understanding*, and *valuing* people. When you do this, you free people up to acknowledge and take ownership of their problems.

Okay, let's get to the heart of this chapter. I'll share a model that can open new areas of understanding about why your people act, respond, and perform the way they do. It helps you understand what's triggering people's responses, actions, and behaviors.

As you look at the Progression of Human Needs Model, here are some ideas to help you understand it better. You'll immediately see lots of applications of these points—both in your own growth and development as well as the growth and development of your associates.

Mull over these points for several minutes and look back at the model.

Progression of Human Needs

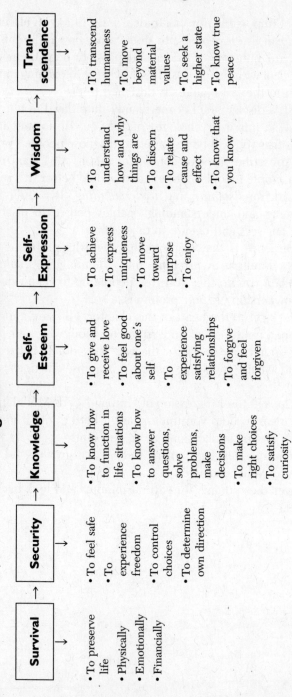

Survival	Security	Knowledge	Self-Esteem	Self-Expression	Wisdom	Transcendence
• To preserve life	• To feel safe	• To know how to function in life situations	• To give and receive love	• To achieve	• To understand how and why things are	• To transcend humanness
• Physically	• To experience freedom	• To know how to answer questions, solve problems, make decisions	• To feel good about one's self	• To express uniqueness	• To discern	• To move beyond material values
• Emotionally	• To control choices	• To make right choices	• To experience satisfying relationships	• To move toward purpose	• To relate cause and effect	• To seek a higher state
• Financially	• To determine own direction	• To satisfy curiosity	• To forgive and feel forgiven	• To enjoy	• To know that you know	• To know true peace

Important Points to Understand from the Model

Here are the points:

1. People are motivated by needs, wants, and values—for hope of gain and relief of pain.
2. Whatever need level people are on, they're primarily concerned with satisfying that specific one and blinded to others.
3. People can be on different need levels in different areas of their lives—areas in lowest need levels will usually dominate and demand greater attention.
4. When a need level is satisfied, people automatically move to the next higher one.
5. People's productivity increases as they satisfy need levels.
6. Self-reliance, willingness to assume responsibility, creativity, motivation, and productivity increase as people move toward higher needs.

Understanding this model and these six points can give you a whole new, comprehensive understanding of people's actions and motivations.

Identify Need Levels Different People Are On

As you listen to your people, and especially as you conduct coaching sessions for them, began to identify what need levels they're on.

To complicate it, and human beings are very complex as you've found out, people can be on different need levels in different areas of their lives. These conflicts cause most of people's problems.

Here are some different areas in which people can be on different need levels.

1. Financial
2. Social
3. Family
4. Relationships
5. Work
6. Spiritual
7. Personal/Health

This does complicate matters, doesn't it?

An employee who's capable and competent suddenly goes through a divorce, and his productivity drops in half for months. A person with low self-esteem constantly torpedoes herself by making error after error. A salesperson on a survival level goes for the quick score rather than building long-term relationships. Someone's teenager suddenly exhibits irrational behavior and a drug problem comes to light. Reorganization causes people to fear for their jobs. So all their activities and decisions are "protect your flanks" responses.

I remember an event in 1980 that turned my business upside down. I had begun my training business in 1965 and had developed several courses that helped people enjoy personal growth and reach new, expanded goals.

I'd been a contributing editor to *Success* magazine, and one year end I was invited to conduct a goal-setting seminar for the staff of the magazine. It was a real honor and I was excited. When the day came, I was even more excited because who should show up but the publisher, W. Clement Stone, himself.

I'd devoured his and Napoleon Hill's books. His *Success Through a Positive Mental Attitude* was the first self-help book I ever read. And it changed my life.

After the seminar, I had dinner with Mr. Stone and he asked to see the things I'd written. I went back to Chicago and spent a whole day with him, showing him all my program materials.

He asked me to work with him three days a week for six months, and I did even though I had my own business. It was a great thrill to be around him, have dinner with him, learn from him. I traveled to England with him working with Boys Clubs directors from around the world. It was a high point of my career.

My own business was growing and we were reinvesting most of our money into developing new programs and never had excess cash. One day, in Chicago, a man whose organization owed us over $600,000 came to see me at the hotel. He said that because of high interest rates and being overleveraged, he was broke and would not be able to pay me. He'd been a very successful, conservative businessman for thirty years, but he went down for the count.

I owed about $250,000 that was secured by this person's receivables.

It was the most devastating event of my business career. It happened so suddenly that I was thrust from a moderately high level of growth and success to a survival level financially.

I scrambled and did everything I could think of just to stay afloat. I sold my courses for about ten cents on the invested dollar. I liquidated equipment and fixtures for as much as I could get—which wasn't much. I let all my staff go, only keeping a part-time secretary. I had no money, no business left, and what seemed like a mountain of debt.

A survival state brought out strengths and creative energies that I didn't know I had. It took every ounce of strength I could muster just to survive! It would take two years to pay off the IRS and creditors. It would take another four years to pay the bank, as interest rates approached 21 percent. It was like trying to fill up a gas guzzler with its motor running.

All my thoughts and efforts were on survival. If you'd attempted to talk to me about long-term planning, or anything like that, I wouldn't have heard a word you said because I was so focused on basic financial survival.

Lower Need Levels Demand Greater Attention

I've learned that the lower the need level we're on, the more it'll demand attention. It'll scream louder than other levels. It'll also create greater stress in our lives. I'd never known stress to the degree that I did when that event happened in 1980.

But, with stress comes learning and discovery. As I've observed people under stress, I've learned that whether they grow and learn or get flattened is determined by their *values* and *achievement drive*.

People with weak, compromisable values will often cut corners and bend rules in order to survive—especially when under strong stress pressure. They don't learn lessons they could have otherwise learned. People with strong positive values take stress head-on and in experiencing it, learn great lessons and grow in ways they could never have otherwise done. Stress and challenges don't necessarily make a person; they reveal who the person is. It was James Allen who wrote, "Circumstances don't make a man. They reveal him to himself."

What's the message for you?

Do you have people who are preoccupied and inattentive? Their minds a thousand miles away? Probably some area of their lives is screaming for attention, occupying their productive thoughts and energy and taking their attention off their jobs.

So, what can you do about this common problem?

How to Help People Get Unstuck

Now, again, I'm not suggesting that you play junior psychologist, but there are some things you can do to help your people get unstuck. They are:

1. Thoroughly understand the Progression of Human Needs Model.

2. Begin conducting the Coaching Process you learned in the previous chapter.

3. Ask questions that get your people talking about and thereby *discovering for themselves* things that are going on in their lives that impact their job performance.

4. Listen to people. *Don't* give advice. Just listen and attempt to understand their feelings.

5. Ask them what they learned and what actions they'll take.

As I've mentioned, there's power in listening for understanding, not to judge a person or give advice. Many times I've listened to people, asking occasional questions that cause them to look deeper within themselves, only to have them smile, relax, and say, "Thank you, you've helped me so much!" All I did was listen nonjudgmentally and try to understand how they felt.

Most of the answers to our challenges are within us—if we're asked the right questions and allowed to verbalize our thoughts and feelings in a nonjudgmental atmosphere.

Your Own Need Levels Influence Your Understanding of Your Associates' Need Levels

Yeah, your own need levels influence your understanding of your associates' need levels. If you are near survival level in some area of your life, it will be difficult for you to focus on other people's needs. It's your own survival or safety needs that will scream for attention. And this is a real problem for many managers—with all the reorganization and downsizing and changes taking place, tremendous trauma terrorizes managers.

Organizational Euthanasia!

"Organizational euthanasia!" That's what one expert calls much of the reorganizational fixes currently being carried out in an attempt to boost the productivity lags of the past twenty-five years.

What's going on? Consider these facts.

- Of the Fortune 500 companies of 1950, only one out of six exists today. Why?

- A 1994 *USA Today* poll revealed that 80 percent of the people interviewed thought that the values and ethical standards had declined in recent years.

- In a study conducted by the American Management Association, only 43 percent of 547 organizations studied that had downsized during the last six years experienced an improvement in profitability.

- Another study revealed that 75 percent of those companies that were downsized believed their performance did *not* improve, and 67 percent reported no increase in productivity.

- Kenneth P. DeMeuse, Paul A. Vanderheiden, and Thomas J. Bergimann, writing for the *Human Resource* magazine, stress that firms which had large-scale layoffs did not show financial improvement. "Rather, their performance continues to decline," they write, "following announcement and at a greater degree than firms that had no layoff announcements."

- A recent Andersen Consulting study revealed that despite all the billions of dollars spent in technology, individual productivity is up only 1 percent since 1982.

What does all this mean?

Put all these facts together and you end with what's called the Productivity Paradox.

The paradox is that despite the vast dollars spent in technology and reorganizations of companies, businesses appear to be no better off than before and in many cases are worse off.

Productivity Plummets!

As companies were traumatized by reorganization, productivity plummeted and paranoia among remaining managers and workers spread like measles in kindergarten. A new illness, "survivor sickness," was introduced to our vocabulary.

This led Dr. Donald E. Rosen, a psychiatrist who directs the Professionals in Crisis Program at the highly respected Menninger Clinic in Topeka, Kansas, to make the following statement: "Victims are lethargic, feel empty, no longer able to take satisfaction in what they once enjoyed." He goes on to say, "They have deep questioning of the value of the tasks they perform."

The bottom line is that they hate to go to work and face the pain.

Like one manager, wracked by the trauma of reorganization, recently told me, "I get up every morning, check the obituaries hoping that I died the night before, and not finding any evidence of my demise, have my wife whack me over the head with a baseball bat—knowing that that's as good as I'll feel all day!"

Daniel Yankelovich, the public-opinion expert, whose organization recently completed a survey of top executives about the results of their reorganizations, must surely have intended understatement when he said, "Most managers don't have as firm a hand on the human aspects of restructuring as they do on finance and technology."

The psychological damage to those loyal employees and managers who had given their lives to the company stores was predictable. Shock, fear, anger, disorientation, depression, aloneness—all followed in a natural order.

Senior executives soothed their corporate consciences by spending big bucks on out-placement help; $700 million in one year alone in the early 1990s.

But out-placement became a joke. I asked several out-placement professionals about the quality of their work. I found out they were forced to get people in the front door and out the back door as quickly as possible as a show of appeasement. As the numbers rose, companies forced them to reduce their costs, which naturally reduced their services and, of course, their effectiveness.

"Survivors," says David Noer, an expert in organizational behavior at the Center for Creative Leadership in Greensboro, North Carolina, "go through a process of psychic numbing that is similar in many ways—although far less shattering—to that of those who have lived through plane crashes and similar disasters."

Among other crippling emotions, survivors feel guilty, like soldiers who lived while their buddies next to them in the foxhole got shot and killed.

One survivor said, "As a result, my employer is getting 10 percent of my former creativity and maybe 50 percent of my energy. I'm the classic employee who quit but still shows up to pick up my paycheck."

Put all these organizational changes in the hopper and you'll see real life demonstrations of the Progression of Human Needs Model's lesson—people scrambling to protect their flanks.

Summing Up

Yes, people do get stuck and unproductive, and you can't help them until you understand what's pressing their buttons and screaming for attention in their lives.

You have circumstances pushing your buttons and screaming for your attention, and it makes the process of understanding other people more difficult.

One of the strongest needs in human nature is to be understood. When you listen nonjudgmentally and try to understand people, you automatically cause them to grow and become better.

Simply understanding people's needs releases power from within them.

I presented to you a Progression of Human Needs Model. It helps you understand why your people act, think, and perform the way they do. Understanding it will strengthen your insights into yourself and others.

Many of your people's low-productivity problems can be solved simply by *listening, understanding,* and *valuing* them. This creates a climate in which your people are free to discover their own answers, as well as see themselves being more productive.

When people move to higher need levels, they grow and become better at what they do.

Organizational change and turmoil creates problems that are understood more by learning about the Progression of Human Needs Model. Understanding these concepts and implementing the Coaching Process in our previous chapter offers new tools to boost your people's productivity.

How to Gain the Most from This Chapter

Pick out several key action points in this chapter that will help you understand where your people are and what's triggering their performance responses.

Follow these suggestions:

1. Read this chapter, come back and scan your notes several times a week.

2. Study and understand the Progression of Human Needs Model. Identify what levels your people might be on. This will help you understand why they act and respond as they sometimes do.

3. Listen to your people, using the model as a filter through which to understand them.

4. Look and listen for clues that might help you understand what areas of a person's life are screaming for attention.

People's performance is almost never a question of knowing what to do or how to do it. There are consistently stronger internal dimensions motivating them.

5. "The Most Important Psychological Discovery of the Century"

Every man is where he is by the law of his being; the thoughts which he has built into his character have brought him there, and in the arrangement of his life there is no element of chance, but all is the result of a law which cannot err.

—JAMES ALLEN

Nothing is more perplexing to a manager than to have a bright and knowledgeable person whose productivity level is sub par. These people exist in almost every organization. Attempting to understand why these people don't produce more, take more initiative, or exhibit stronger achievement drive drives managers up bananas trees.

Close to 20 percent of your people fall naturally into this category, with others on the border. The truth is that everyone's performance is controlled, not by what they know, but by what they internally think they *should* be doing; or what they're *capable* of doing. Deep within each person's emotional makeup lies a deeply seated individual belief system. This belief system—this self-image or mental paradigm—controls all their actions, feelings, behaviors, and abilities.

A person's performance will always be consistent with what they internally believe they *can* or *should* be producing. It can't go beyond their inner beliefs about what they think they're capable of doing. Many of your attempts to get them to improve will fail until their perception about themselves changes.

"The most important psychological discovery of the century" explains Dr. Maxwell Maltz in his classic, *Psycho-Cybernetics*, "is the discovery of the 'self-image.' Whether we realize it or not, each of us carries about with us a mental blueprint or picture of ourselves. It may be vague and ill-defined to our own conscious gaze. In fact, it may not be consciously recognizable at all. But it is there, complete down to the last detail.

"This self-image," he continues, "becomes a golden key to living a better life because of two very important discoveries:

1. "All your actions, feelings, behavior—even your abilities are always consistent with your self-image.

2. "The self-image can be changed."

Understanding the power of a person's self-image and that it is changeable raises many questions. Like: Where does a person's self-image reside? What creates it? How can it be changed? What happens when it does change?

In a moment, I'll share with you a model I've developed. Hopefully, this will help you gain new insights into why people produce on the level that they do, as well as understand why the training and incentives that you've used didn't achieve long-term increases.

Human nature hasn't changed throughout history. We simply have failed to understand it beyond surface levels. It was one hundred years ago that Dr. William James wrote, "The greatest discovery of my generation is that men can change their lives by changing their attitudes of mind."

This raises a significant question that we miss if we only deal with it intellectually. It's "What did he mean when he said, 'attitudes of mind'?"

Later, J. F. Newton wrote, "It is not necessary to get away from human nature but to alter its inner attitude of mind and heart."

"Attitude of mind and heart?" What does that mean?

And, then, Bruce Bliven wrote, "Perhaps the most important lesson the world has learned in the past fifty years is that it is not true that 'human nature is unchangeable.' Human nature, on the contrary, can be changed with the greatest ease and to the utmost possible extent. If in this lies huge potential danger, it also contains some of the brightest hopes that we have for the future of mankind."

Our Logical Minds Fail to Understand the Illogic of Human Nature

Human nature is anything but logical.

It was Anatole France who remarked, "It is human nature to think wisely and act foolishly."

The main reason we fail to understand human nature is that we are inspecting it through logical, linear, rational lenses. And when people fail to live up to our logical paradigms, we blame them instead of changing our frameworks of understanding. When we recognize that people's actions will usually follow illogical patterns, we develop different viewpoints and measurements of understanding people.

I could never understand why a friend lived in a small two-bedroom home in a run-down section of town, when truthfully he was bright, articulate, handsome, and had a good personality. Then it dawned on me that I was seeing totally different things in him than he saw in himself. Logic, facts, reality meant little to him. Because of a bitter failure in his life, he believed he was a failure. And he carried this self-evaluation with him to his premature grave.

So, as we move into this chapter, let me suggest that you

plan to suspend logic as you evaluate and try to understand your people. Instead, plan to discover a predominant illogic in their actions, responses, and behavior. The basis of most mis-understandings comes because we expect people to conform to our logical views of how they should react.

As Alfred North Whitehead once remarked, "It takes a very unusual mind to make an analysis of the obvious." Or, said another way, it takes a very *illogical* mind to *logically* under-stand the *illogic*. (I'm not even sure *I* understand what I've just written.)

Granted that understanding human nature presents many challenges, let me share a model that jumped on a flip chart one day when I was conducting a seminar. It was one of those rare moments when my subconscious kicked stuff up to my conscious and caused me to understand new levels of what had previously been hidden from me.

Three Dimensions That Impact Human Performance

That we are multidimensional beings isn't exactly new knowl-edge. Wise people have hinted at it for centuries. We just don't know what to do about it. Let me share the following Human Behavior Model that explains it well.

First, let me suggest that there are three separate, although interrelated, dimensions within us. They are the:

1. Intellectual
2. Emotional
3. Creative/Unconscious

Remember, they are separate yet interconnected. This, of course, is a paradox, but then, human behavior seldom follows a consistent path. We are all paradoxes—bundles of contradic-tions.

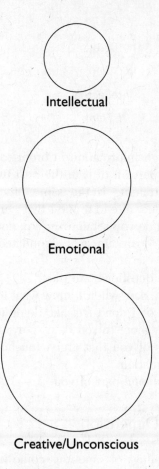

Intellectual

Emotional

Creative/Unconscious

The Intellectual Dimension

The *Intellectual* dimension is the rational, conscious, cognitive, wide-awake part of us. We'll call it the *"I Think."*

This is the part that learns information, remembers facts and figures, and sees the world in a black-or-white, cause-and-effect manner. Most of our education is directed toward this part of us. We sit in classrooms, listen to lectures, read books at night, and take tests occasionally. If we remember enough facts to pass the tests, we are considered educated. But how often have

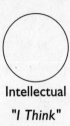

Intellectual

"I Think"

you saved up enough information in order to pass a test, and then released 94.6 percent of it in the next twenty-one days?

Most so-called training is the same process—listen to a speech, watch a video, attend a one-, two-, or three-day seminar. But how much do you retain over a period of time or how much of what you do retain gets assimilated and applied in your actions?

Not comfortable questions, are they?

Or, why are there days when I know what to do, but I either don't *want* to do it or I don't *feel* like doing it?

There's obviously more to you than your intellectual nature, and there are parts of you that aren't touched by knowledge, education, or information.

There's the *Emotional* part of you.

The Emotional Dimension

Where do your feelings or emotions come from? Why when things are going well do you sometimes have a sense of fore-

Emotional

"I Feel"

boding? Why, when you are hip-deep in alligators and roaring Bengal tigers do you often feel surprisingly positive and confident and energized?

Studies have shown that around 15 percent of our success on the job is due to knowledge and skills and 85 percent is due to emotional factors—feelings, attitudes, beliefs.

You've noticed that with your people, haven't you? Often, the least bright and brainy are the most productive. People with positive, can-do attitudes who are happy and whose beliefs and values are in sync with your organization's vision, mission, and core values generally produce more. Specific attitudes or thought patterns produce specific results. It's cause and effect. And, often, some of your less bright people are your most productive.

Who can make sense of this? Hopefully, you'll make more sense of it after digesting this chapter.

Where do your attitudes or feelings come from? Why do you feel up one day and down the next? How much does an attitude or feeling weigh? What shape or color is it? How do you measure it? Obviously, these logical questions don't fit.

In order to understand where your emotions come from, let's think about the third dimension—the *Creative/Unconscious* part of you.

The Creative/Unconscious Dimension

The *Creative/Unconscious* dimension is the deep, profound part that houses your values, self-image, feelings of worth, view of your own possibilities, Life Force, and your spiritual makeup.

This part of you is the "I Am." It's *who* you see yourself being. It's what you think you're capable of achieving, earning, producing. It's the creative part of you that, once you learn to access it, helps you make new things out of old elements. Great inventors, painters, poets, and musicians have discovered this part of themselves and learned how to access it. Thomas Edison

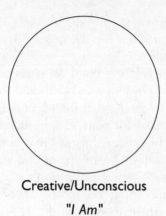

Creative/Unconscious

"I Am"

denied to a reporter that he was a "creative genius," explaining that he had simply learned to draw from his creative unconscious.

It's the part of you that is working at 3:00 A.M. You wake up, and when you're 2 percent awake and 98 percent still asleep, an idea that you've been searching for explodes in your mind. Or you wake up while dreaming, and you don't know whether the dream is reality or reality is a dream. You then discover that something is going on inside you while you're asleep. But who can understand it?

It's in this part of you that your powerful Goal-Seeking Mechanism exists and steers you toward goals. It's the power that translates your dominant thoughts into physical reality.

In his classic *As a Man Thinketh*, James Allen, the English minister, wrote this wise observation: "The soul attracts that which it secretly harbors; that which it loves and also that which it fears; it reaches the height of its cherished aspirations; it falls to the level of its unchastened desires—and circumstances are the means by which the soul receives its own."

This Creative Mechanism can operate as a success mechanism or a failure mechanism, depending on the kind of goals we feed it. As we set positive, productive goals, this mechanism works to make them a reality. Set negative, destructive goals, and it works to make those a reality. Our values and self-esteem level assess goals and screen them through our sense of right and wrong, possible or impossible.

This *Creative/Unconscious* houses our Life Force—the essence of who we are. Dr. Joseph B. Rhine of Duke University fame referred to an "extra physical" dimension within people. Dr. Hans Selye, early pioneer in the study of stress, referred to a nonphysical part of us he called "adaptive energy." Dr. Carl Jung referred to it in his theory of "synychronicity." Dr. Maxwell Maltz called it the Life Force. The Élan Vital. He used to tell me, "The energy that heals a wound is the same energy which keeps all our other body parts functioning—regulates our heartbeat, pulse rate, temperature, lymphatic flow and growth."

In the seven years I worked with Dr. Maltz before his death in 1975, I heard him often quote Dubois, the French surgeon, "The surgeon dresses the wound, God heals it." I once asked him what was the most amazing thing he'd ever seen. He replied, "Watching a wound heal. Watching God at work!"

He believed, as I do, that God, the ultimate Creator, created humankind in His own image as the Scriptures tell us. And because we're created in God's image, and as we discover that part of ourselves that's been created in His image, we discover our own Creative Mechanism. I believe that this bit of Divinity resides in our *Creative/Unconscious* part. I believe this "Spirit in the inner man," as the Apostle Paul describes it, lives on after death. It's the deepest expression of my essence—created by a Divine Creator to be creative and to express that creativity through the unique talents He's given us.

Individual Productivity Comes from the "I Am" Dimension

Individual productivity reflects what's happening in your people's "I Am" dimension more than in their "I Think."

Please read this preceding statement again. Chew on it for a few moments. Notice the following drawing.

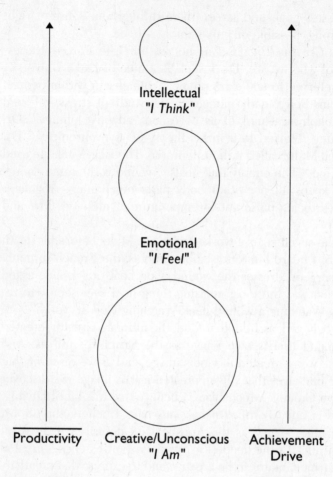

Intellectual
"*I Think*"

Emotional
"*I Feel*"

Productivity   Creative/Unconscious   Achievement
                          "*I Am*"   Drive

Accomplishment   Self-Motivation

We often mistakenly assume that knowledge begets productivity. It doesn't! Sure, we have to know lots of stuff—product, activity, industry, competitive and technological knowledge. We must know as much as we can. But your people will not be highly productive just because they know information!

Think I'm misstating my case? Look around your organization at the people who have the most technical or job knowledge. Are they your most productive ones? Maybe some are, but most aren't—at least in the organizations with which I've worked—especially sales or customer-service people.

Achievement drive, self-motivation, energy—all are released from your people's "I Am" dimensions. It's *released* from within, not poured in from without. We get this all mixed up as we attempt to "motivate" people; but as I've said before, you can't motivate people. You can only create a climate wherein people motivate themselves. You'll only be effective if your people want to be self-motivated. If "being more productive" fits into the framework of their self-images; if "having more" or "doing better" or "producing more" is consistent with the blueprint in their "I Am," they'll be motivated and will release significant new levels of achievement drive.

That's a tough lesson for managers (especially driver types) to learn. Which, on a broader scale, is why individual productivity has been flat for thirty years despite all the new technological advances.

Heavy stuff, isn't it? I know you have lots of questions. A couple are, "Well, if my people's 'I Am' dimension controls their productivity, then what creates it, and can it be changed?"

Let's answer these questions.

How Are People's "I Am" Dimensions Formed?

Basically, people's "I Am" dimensions are programmed by their responses to the whole of their life experiences. Life experiences like:

1. Emotional state of mothers.
2. Love, stimulation, and nurturing of an infant.
3. Early environment.
4. Successes and failures.
5. Support systems.
6. Values and beliefs of parents.
7. Peers in formative years.

8. Genetics.

9. Environmental values and mores.

10. And something else . . . known and unknown.

At some point people "buy" the "who I think I am," and then play it out in their lives. Their actions, feelings, abilities, and behavior will be consistent with what they've accepted as truth in their "I Am."

These beliefs will then powerfully influence their emotions and life responses. If people have had a preponderance of positive life situations, if they've experienced love, healthy relationships, strong support systems, and an excess of successes over defeats; then chances are there's a congruence, within their "I Am." This state will produce positive emotions of love, joy, enthusiasm, confidence, benevolence, forgiveness.

Look at it like this. Let's let the parallel lines in the following "I Am" represent congruence, harmony, order, peace and then see what emotions are produced.

Then, let's consider the opposite. Let's think of some emotions that are the result of negative experiences like conflict, abuse, disharmony, turmoil, low self-esteem, and confusion.

Note the following factors in the "I Am" and how they express themselves in the "I Feel."

How Positive Emotions Are Created

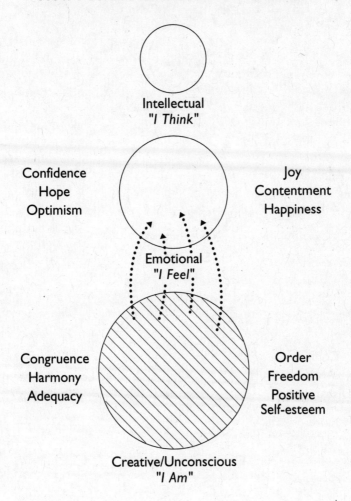

How Negative Emotions Are Created

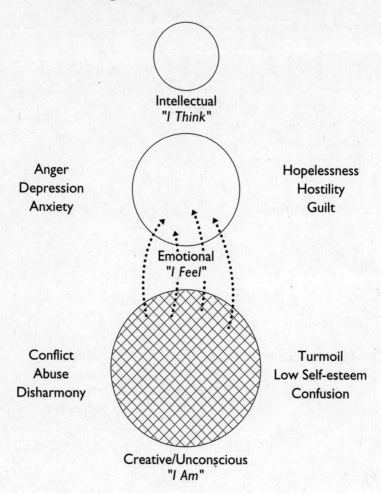

How Your People's "I Am" Dimension Is Influenced

Let's recap.

1. Your people's "I Am" dimension influences their productivity and performance.
2. It's been formed by their responses to their life experiences. You can't do anything to change their past, but you can understand it.
3. Their "I Am" produces their emotions, which affects their job performance more than does what they know.
4. People will only produce more when growth occurs in their "I Am" dimension.

So, the question is, "Well then how can I help build my people's "I Am" so they'll produce more?"

That's the *big* question and, incidentally, what this book is about.

Factors That Influence Your People's "I Am"

Here are some personal and organizational factors that influence your people's "I Am." Regardless of what's currently in their "I Am" dimensions, there are strategies that you can begin doing to help build them.

Personal

1. Setting and reaching new goals
2. Positive reinforcement
3. Nonjudgmental listening
4. Supportive personal environment
5. Unconditional acceptance
6. Visualizing successes

Organizational

1. Shared purpose and vision
2. Feel job role has meaning
3. Authentic mentors
4. Positive coaching and counseling that rewards results
5. Job security
6. Generating value for customers

Reflect and you'll see that a great deal of what's happened in organizational changes in the last few years strikes right at the heart of people's "I Am." You'll also see that radical changes must be made to create organizational foundations that support people's growth; and how the Coaching and Counseling Model that I shared in chapter 3 can help you build people at their "I Am" level.

Values, Beliefs, Congruence

One of the deepest needs within people is for congruence, order, harmony, peace. Inner congruence occurs when people's actions match their values and beliefs. When there is inner congruence, people produce more. When there are inner conflicts, productivity drops. Obviously, corporate executives don't consider this as they plan logical cuts and layoffs—organizational slash-and-burn tactics.

Theory of Cognitive Dissonance

Dr. Leon Festinger of Stanford University coined the term "cognitive dissonance" to explain a common phenomenon.

Cognitive means the mind or the way we think. Dissonance means conflict. So, "cognitive dissonance" literally means having mental conflicts.

Basically, the Theory of Cognitive Dissonance means this:

· *When people are asked to perform in a way that's inconsistent with their values, beliefs, perceived skills or abilities, a dissonance or conflict occurs that inhibits their performance.*

Here are some situations that cause people to experience "cognitive dissonance."

1. Don't feel aligned with the organization's purpose.
2. Values conflict with manager's values.
3. They're asked to perform in a way that doesn't match their skills, abilities, or knowledge.
4. They're asked to do activities that are inconsistent with their values.
5. They're on different need levels in different areas of their lives that create conflicts.
6. They're given production quotas but aren't given adequate training and tools.
7. Managers telling them that they should be producing on a higher level, but their internal beliefs won't allow them to accept these higher possibilities.
8. Managers using motivational strategies that are purely externally driven.
9. Personal relationship conflicts.
10. Lack of job security.

Does it sound complicated? Of course it does! People are extremely complicated. And while you'll never be able to understand people completely, you can significantly increase their performance by understanding their behavior.

Summing Up

I've stressed that people aren't productive just because they have knowledge or abilities. Their productivity depends on how they see themselves—what they think they are capable of within the framework of who they are.

I shared a model of the three dimensions within you.

1. Intellectual, "I Think"
2. Emotional, "I Feel"
3. Creative/Unconscious, "I Am"

You understood that people's emotions often overpower their knowledge. "I know I shouldn't eat that chocolate pie, but I *want* it!" "I know I shouldn't smoke and that it will kill me, but I just can't give it up!" "I know I should work harder, but I may not be around next month!" So our emotions often over-rule our logic or knowledge.

You learned where your people's emotions come from and that they can be changed by reprogramming their "I Am" dimension.

As you understand this model, you'll immediately see how everything in this book fits together to give you the tools to build your people. You build them by helping strengthen their "I Am" dimension.

This is a whole new paradigm of leadership thinking. It represents the shift from managing people to leading them. From either being policemen or baby-sitters to being coaches.

I challenge you to absorb the concepts in this chapter before going on to the next ones. Then, relate this model to the two previous chapters—the coaching chapter and the one about human needs. Tie them together.

This will give you much more insight into people, and as you begin to assimilate and apply the concepts, you'll begin to enjoy significant increases in individual productivity.

Remember, the key to higher productivity is building people at their "I Am" level.

How to Gain the Most from This Chapter

Focus on this chapter for a week, absorb the material, read it several times, underline and make notes on your pages.
In addition, please do the following activities:

1. Estimate what percentage of your people are stuck on plateaus.
2. Begin to try to understand what people's behavior, productivity, or actions reveal about their inner belief systems about themselves.
3. Study the three dimensions of the Human Behavior Model. Understand each dimension and its role in influencing your people's behavior.
4. Reflect on what life experiences or self-perceptions have impacted your "I Am" dimension.
5. Review the Factors That Influence Your People's "I Am" and choose one or two ideas to practice this week.
6. Study Dr. Leon Festinger's Theory of Cognitive Dissonance and see if you can identify work force conflicts that may cause lower performance in your people.

People will hook it up and work their buns off for you when they sense you know where you're going, value them, and depend on them to help you get there!

6. "If I'm a Leader, Who's Succeeding Because of Me?"

Faith in the ability of a leader is of slight service unless it be united with faith in his justice.

—GEORGE W. GOETHALS

Great leaders are very rare! Partly because they're paradoxes—they exhibit two qualities that appear almost conflicting. People who have one don't always have the other. Highly effective leaders have these two traits in *balance*.

What are these two traits?

1. Sensitivity to people, and
2. Goal directedness

Let's think about these two qualities.

Sensitivity to people gives you strong empathic skills—the ability to tune in to people, really listen, understand what they say and how they feel.

Leaders have highly developed intuitive skills—they seem to know what people are thinking. They're often able to sense people's responses before they happen. Many can almost crawl into other people's skins and experience their feelings and emotions. It's empathy. Rapport. Feeling with others.

Goal directedness is the ability to set clear goals or objectives, then marshal the people and resources necessary to achieve desirable results. These people are bottom-line oriented. They believe that results are what counts but that results are to be achieved within frameworks of values, ethics, honesty, and integrity.

Goal-directed leaders, managers, or coaches exhibit strong positive assertiveness and have high expectations of results. They hold people accountable. They have high energy and achievement drive. They're highly motivated to achieve results. They're decision makers.

Now, let's look at a model that contrasts these two qualities. Notice that four quadrants emerge. I call these

Quadrant 1   Friend
Quadrant 2   Leader
Quadrant 3   Follower
Quadrant 4   Boss

Manager Styles Model

	High	
Sensitivity to People	Quadrant 1 High Sensitivity/Low Goal Directedness **Friend**	Quadrant 2 High Sensitivity/High Goal Directedness **Leader**
	Quadrant 3 Low Sensitivity/Low Goal Directedness **Follower**	Quadrant 4 Low Sensitivity/High Goal Directedness **Boss**
	Low High	

Goal Directedness

Here are some characteristics of each style.

Friend

Characteristics:

- Relationship driven
- Social, amiable
- Listens selectively
- Sincere, caring
- Low assertiveness
- Loyal
- Needs approval of others
- Low goal directedness
- Difficulty with decisions
- Avoids confrontations
- Fears loss of social approval
- Fun-loving

Leader

Characteristics:

- Clarity of organizational or team purpose, direction, goals
- Self-Confident
- Works through people to solve problems
- Values driven
- Decisive
- Builds people
- Results-oriented/respect for people balance
- Energetic
- Highly intuitive
- Leads by example
- Highly responsible
- Excellent listener

Follower

Characteristics:

- Low energy
- Nonassertive
- Unclear goals
- Avoids responsibility for results
- Indecisive
- Not creative
- Seeks security
- Process focused

Boss

Characteristics:

- Clarity of own personal goals
- Self-Confident to arrogant
- Assertive
- Insensitive to people's feelings or thoughts
- Very decisive
- High energy

Characteristics:

- Avoids confrontation
- Swayed by stronger people
- Avoids accountability
- Weak initiative

Characteristics:

- Autocratic, confrontational
- Self-Focused
- Poor listener
- Results-oriented
- Highly responsible
- Fears loss of power

As you look at this model, let me make several points about it.

1. Few people are single-quadrant styles. Most managers have traits that fall into two different categories (maybe even three), but usually one quadrant will be dominant.

2. Moving into quadrant 2 usually involves work and effort. Not many people naturally have that balance.

3. Quadrant 2 isn't a level that's completely achieved. It's a lifelong challenge.

As you've probably observed by now, moving into quadrant 2 is a growth process. Few people naturally balance these two traits. Most people would have either sensitivity to people or goal directedness as natural traits and have to especially work on the other. Said another way, people with these two traits in balance originally had one but had to work to develop the other.

Take a few moments and score yourself on the following assessment to get a general idea of where you fit on the model. You've read these twelve descriptors of leadership in a previous chapter, but now let's think of them in a different way.

Check off the most descriptive statement under each of the following traits of leadership.

Manager Styles Assessment

1. Vision

    a. My purpose is to enjoy my work and develop relationships with people.

    b. My purpose is to help my organization carry out its mission, achieve profitability, and create a meaningful work environment.

    c. My purpose is to run my department well and make sure we achieve our profit and production goals.

2. Charisma

    a. People like me, but they don't see me as an "out-front" leader-type person.

    b. My concern for our people's welfare combined with my clear focus on our objectives causes people to want to follow me.

    c. I'm the boss and people know they'd better do what I tell them.

3. Character

    a. I want to get along with people, have them like me, and just go with the flow.

    b. I will get the job done without violating the rights of others or compromising my values.

    c. I'll get the job done even if I have to bend some rules or twist some arms.

4. Responsibility

    a. I do not want the responsibility that a lot of jobs entail.

    b. I accept responsibility to reach my objective within the framework of our core values.

    c. I accept responsibility to get results, whatever it takes.

5. Planning

a. I'm not very good at planning. I'm more of a people person than a detail person.
b. I realize the value of good plans and carefully involve others in that activity.
c. I find that our plans are made better and faster if I make them and then tell people what I want.

6. Social Skills

a. I get along well with people and having friends is one of the most important things for me.
b. I value people's input and am able to listen to them without bias and work with them toward problem resolutions.
c. I am so busy that I don't have a lot of time to listen to people, and I find we get more done when I handle most of the problems.

7. Achievement Drive

a. There's a lot more to life than just work. I see my job mainly as a way to make a living.
b. I am highly energized to get as much done through people as I can, within the framework of our core values and ethics.
c. I am highly competitive and will not allow anything or anyone to get in my way.

8. Emotional Stability

a. I avoid confrontations because I don't want to make enemies or deal with touchy issues.
b. I expect ups and downs and can treat difficult situations as growth experiences and work through them without losing emotional control.

c. When people don't do what I want them to do it drives me nuts, and I let them know my feelings in no uncertain terms.

9. Tolerance for Ambiguity

a. I don't like having to work with annoying people or having to handle frustrating experiences.
b. I deal with frustrating experiences in a patient way, keeping my eye focused ahead on our organizational objectives.
c. I can handle lots of challenges, but occasionally I get fed up and I can really blow my stack!

10. Decisiveness

a. I tend to get bogged down in making decisions because I'm afraid of offending some of the people involved.
b. I am able to involve others in assessing situations and then move to quick decisions once all the facts are understood.
c. I can size up situations, make excellent decisions myself, and direct others to carry them out.

11. Delegation

a. I am not very good at telling people what to do and then following up to see if they've done it.
b. I am able to fit different tasks and objectives to competent people and periodically inspect their performance.
c. When I give people a job to do, they know they'd better get it done.

12. Positive Outlook

a. I enjoy working with people, but I don't enjoy the responsibility of being a manager.

b. I believe that, working through my team and following our core values, we can achieve our goals.

c. The only way I can reach my goals is for those people to get off their duffs and work harder.

Now, as you might guess, your responses to these questions probably indicate that your natural inclinations fall in quadrant 1, 2, or 4. I'm omitting reference to quadrant 3 because rarely would people working their way into management or leadership positions fall in this category. They would never be reading a book like this.

After scoring yourself in the Twelve Traits of Leadership, count up the number of 1's, 2's and 4's that you have. Then shade in squares in each quadrant. Obviously, a's are in quadrant 1, b's in 2, and c's in 4.

Friend   **Leader**

Follower   **Boss**

Okay, now be honest with yourself. No one's perfect, so don't skew your responses to resemble Alexander the Great or your image of the greatest leader of all time. Hey, if you were perfect, you'd have no more room to grow; and growth is what makes life thrilling. Beside, you'd certainly not need to read a book like this; and just think of the poverty you'd force me into.

So, take a few moments and check off or shade in a square in each quadrant for each selection you made in the questionnaire. Chances are you'll check off squares in each of the three quadrants, with a greater percentage in two.

As I've indicated before, quadrant 2 Leader is a hybrid—the balance of two sometimes conflicting styles. Most of us aren't natural leaders. Our natural state is either to be a Follower, Friend, or Boss. Our leadership skills generally develop as we recognize the traits necessary for us to lead people. Yeah, maybe there are a few natural-born leaders, but most work to develop the necessary skills.

Developing Leadership Skills

I'm assuming that you are intent on developing stronger skills in quadrant 2. Developing balanced leadership skills will keep most of us busy for a bunch of years to come. The more I develop these skills, the more apparent it is that there are greater dimensions I still need to work on. The more I learn, the more I learn there is to learn.

In the balance of this chapter, I'll give you some ideas and suggestions that can help you develop a balance of

1. Sensitivity to people, and
2. Goal directedness.

Let me stress that this isn't an *intellectual* process. Simply reading and understanding these ideas won't really help much. The suggestions I'll give you are meant to be *experienced*. You must take action and practice them in real life, with real people, in real situations.

It is when you, as one of my earlier mentors, W. Clement Stone, advised,

1. *Recognize* success principles.
2. *Relate* them to your life roles.
3. *Assimilate* them into your actions and ultimately habits, and
4. *Apply* them unconsciously in your everyday life.

After you read this chapter to get an idea of the content, then pick out two or three actions you can begin practicing. I also suggest that after finishing this book, you come back and spend three weeks on this chapter—practicing specific actions I'll share with you.

When these actions become automatic responses, you'll see your leadership effectiveness expand. It's with focus, practice, self-evaluation, and time that you develop automatic responses. Again, simply reading this and intellectually processing the information will not help you transform these ideas into your habits and automatic responses.

Sensitivity to People

In this section, we'll explore some time-honored communication principles such as empathy, intuition, social perception, and nonjudgmental listening; practical skills that will help you understand people.

But, before we do this, let me share some beliefs about people.

1. People have untapped potential that, if discovered, can significantly increase their productivity and self-fulfillment.

2. People produce more when managers respect them and expect the best from them.

3. People will generally produce more when they feel their jobs have meaning and that they count for something in the overall scope of things.

4. People, generally, want to do what's right, and are internally rewarded when they do.

5. A positive belief in people produces a reciprocity wherein people want to do their best for their leaders.

If these beliefs about people match your values and core beliefs and if you accept them as the best guides for leading and enabling people, then the following suggestions will make sense to you.

These actions, when practiced, will help you develop greater skill in understanding people, strengthen your intuitive abilities, and cultivate a greater "sixth sense" about people.

1. Listen to people without biases.

2. Take on the role of the other person.

3. Listen with your eyes and feelings.

4. Reflect back to people their own feelings and ideas.

Let's think about each of these, remembering the advice of Dr. Carl Rogers, the father of modern-day nondirective counseling. "The most powerful persuasive force in interpersonal relations," he wrote, "is the ability to first of all be able to perceive how another person feels, then to take on the other person's role in imagination and reflect his own feelings back to him." In other words, put yourself in the other person's shoes and then express back to him or her how you think you'd feel if you were in his or her shoes.

Listen to People Without Bias

Let me repeat that one of people's strongest needs is for others to listen to them—to what they say, what they think, who they are—in an accepting, nonjudgmental way. Psychological value, communicated to another person, moves quickly to the "I Am" part of that person. They are subconsciously touched and are instinctively impelled to return this same value to you.

Listening without bias doesn't mean that you agree with what a person says. It simply means that you value the person . . . as a person! When this deeper level of communication occurs, there is an unconscious response of reciprocity by the other person. Their reaction to us becomes more positive. We have given value to them, and they're instinctively impelled to return it to us.

Take on the Role of the Other Person

Empathy is not only the ability to listen and understand other people, it's also the skill of crawling into another person's way of thinking. To understand what they're feeling, thinking, how and why they view the world as they do.

It's the advice you were given years ago. "Put yourself in the other person's shoes." It's taking on the other's role in imagination. It's asking, "How do they see things as contrasted with how I see them?"

The following test can give you an indication of your sensitivity to people or your empathic skills. It allows you to:

1. Rate yourself in several key areas.
2. Rate other people as you see them.
3. Rate other people as you think they would rate themselves, and
4. Rate yourself as you think others would rate you.

I'm suggesting that you think about how you see yourself, how you see others, how you think they see themselves, and how you think they see you. Hang in with me. I realize this requires some mental gymnastics, but the results can be very insightful.

First, photocopy the following Empathic Assessment and give a copy and instructions to another person, one who knows you. Ask this person to score you and herself or himself as directed. You will both fill it in, answering all four questions. You're rating yourself and them. They're rating themselves and you.

Empathic Assessment

Confident	5 4 3 2 1 0	0 1 2 3 4 5	Worried
Happy	5 4 3 2 1 0	0 1 2 3 4 5	Sad
Listens	5 4 3 2 1 0	0 1 2 3 4 5	Dominates
Outgoing	5 4 3 2 1 0	0 1 2 3 4 5	Introverted
Friendly	5 4 3 2 1 0	0 1 2 3 4 5	Distant
Excited	5 4 3 2 1 0	0 1 2 3 4 5	Bored
Optimistic	5 4 3 2 1 0	0 1 2 3 4 5	Pessimistic
Leader	5 4 3 2 1 0	0 1 2 3 4 5	Follower
Other-Centered	5 4 3 2 1 0	0 1 2 3 4 5	Self-Centered
Positive Attitude	5 4 3 2 1 0	0 1 2 3 4 5	Negative Attitude

Please do the following four steps.

Step 1—Place a check mark (√) at the point that *you'd rate yourself* in each of these traits that describe you.

Step 2—Place a dot (.) at the point that *you'd rate another specific person* in each of the traits that describe them.

Step 3—Place an (X) at the point that *you* think that *this other person would rate himself or herself.*

Step 4—Place an asterisk (∗) at the point *you think the other person would rate you.*

As you receive the assessment back from the other person, compare your ratings. Here are some ideas.

1. The closer you rate others *as you think they'll rate themselves* (Step 3) to how closely they *actually rate themselves* (Step 1) shows greater empathy or intuition.

2. The closer you think *they would rate you* (Step 4) compared to *how they rated* you (Step 2) shows greater empathic skills.

Now, let me say that this isn't designed to be an accurate assessment of your skills or traits. It is simply to see how *you think others see you* compared to how they actually do. Also, it's to discover *how you think they see themselves* compared to how they actually do.

This is just a simple way to crawl inside another person's mind and see how closely what you think they think matches what they actually think.

Listen with Your Eyes and Feelings

Intuition, empathy, rapport, a sixth sense—all allow us to transcend words and hear with emotional ears what people are saying.

People don't always say with words what they're really attempting to say. There are other ways of speaking that transcend words. Their actual words and what they're trying to communicate are not always synonymous. Dr. Albert Mehrabian of UCLA aptly said it years ago when he published a report called "Communication Effectiveness." He said that communication effectiveness depends:

7% on the words we say
38% on the tone of voice
55% on the nonverbals.

Although this study was done several years ago, it's still relevant.

So, as you listen to people, listen to more than their words. Listen to tone of voice, gestures, body language, listen to their feelings and emotions—their energy.

Reflect Back to People Their Own Feelings and Ideas

You can do this, after you've listened and understood people, by paraphrasing their ideas back to them; by adopting the same tone and pacing; by mirroring the body language they exhibit; by touching people to show understanding; by verbalizing understanding. Like, "I see." "I understand what you're saying." "I understand how you feel."

Remember, again, that it's not a matter of *agreeing* or *disagreeing* with them. It's a matter of *understanding* them. There's a big difference. I can seek to understand a person with whom I totally disagree.

Many controlling, assessing, perfectionistic people think they have to *agree* or *disagree* with others. When they disagree with what others think, they feel a need to reject the whole person, to "set them straight"—to challenge them and change them. Obviously there are times when it's appropriate to challenge people and their ideas. In building people and helping them become more productive, you'll spend most of your time listening and developing rapport. It's wisdom that knows the right time for confrontation.

Okay, these are some ideas about developing greater sensitivity to people. Now, let's think about ways to develop stronger goal directedness.

Goal Directedness

Goal directedness is the orientation that stresses getting results and making things happen. In its natural state, this trait can be the opposite of sensitivity to people. As I've mentioned before, it's usually through work and effort that people develop a balance of the two.

Here are some practical actions you can take to increase your goal directedness.

1. Ask yourself, "What measurable, bottom-line results or outcomes do I want to happen?"
2. Ask, "What do I have to do to make these happen?" (plans, people, resources, skills)
3. Mentally dwell on the rewards you'll enjoy when you make them happen.
4. Say the self-motivator several times each day, "A leader builds people and gets results!"

Developing a Results Orientation

Before you can increase your ability to get results, you must develop a results orientation. The belief that results are what count must guide you.

One of the reasons why there aren't many real leaders is that few people are results-oriented. Most people are process-focused. Their orientation is to do their job or to complete a process. They see their purpose as doing jobs, not how the job function impacts results or objectives.

Just last week I was conducting a seminar for a group of educators. One man who has a Ph.D. and is in a leadership position in a university made a statement that almost took my knees out from under me. He said, "In everything it is the process that's important, not the result." He went on to refer to results-oriented people as "Machiavellian."

At first I thought he was joking, but when I looked at him it was obvious that he was serious.

He was so emphatic about his beliefs that I caught myself wanting to "straighten him out" in the same direct way as he'd said it. But, of course, I didn't. I just listened to him and tried to understand what he was saying. No one in the room challenged him, so we moved on.

How'd you like someone like that running your department?

What we get paid depends on how much we get done through people. Try the previous four suggestions and see how, in time, your goal directedness increases. As you do these actions, keep track of your income, position, or the level of respect others have for your abilities. See how they increase as you cause more goals to be reached.

It may not be discernible in the short term, but over the long haul you'll clearly see your income and rewards climb as you engender greater results.

Summing Up

In this chapter I've shared some ideas about what makes great leaders great. I mentioned two traits that highly effective leaders seem to have in balance. They are

1. Sensitivity to people, and
2. Goal directedness.

These traits are almost contrasting; few people have them in balance; the people who do probably worked hard on one or the other in order to have both. I suggested some strategies or action guides that will help you strengthen either or both these traits.

I shared with you a couple of assessments that can help you understand where you now are and to what areas you might want to give attention.

I suggested that moving into quadrant 2 is a lifelong process. It's a commitment to continual development—realizing that it's not a destination but an ongoing quest for excellence. In my experience, the more I develop leadership qualities, the more I discover that there's more to develop. The more I learn, the more I learn that there is more to learn.

How to Gain the Most from This Chapter

I'm sure that by now you are discovering the power of focused attention and are benefiting from your weekly concentration on a chapter. Keep it up.

Continue to read, digest, underline sentences, and take action on my suggestions. In addition do the following.

1. Thoroughly digest the Manager Styles Model, studying the characteristics of each quadrant.

2. Score yourself on the Manager Styles Assessment and shade in the appropriate number of boxes in each quadrant.

3. Review the action guides for developing greater sensitivity to people and fill in the Empathic Assessment.

4. Practice the action guides for developing stronger goal directedness.

5. As you practice the action guides, you'll have more insights. Write them down as they pop into your mind.

People will go all out for you when you understand their uniqueness, listen through their ears and see the world through the same lenses that they're viewing it.

7. "If You Don't Understand Me, How Can You Lead Me?"

> *People are generally better persuaded by the reasons which they have themselves discovered than by those which have come from the minds of others.*
>
> —Pascal

"He drove me up a wall of impatience and frustration," a client told me about one of his people. "Everything I did to motivate him only seemed to stress *him* out, and then ruin my day. He seemed to have no motivation. Wouldn't assume responsibility. Couldn't see the big picture."

On and on this manager went, venting his frustrations.

It was a classic case of two different styles of people not understanding each other; and as a result, not communicating effectively. I understood him and identified with his frustrations. He was a bottom-line, results-oriented person who saw the big picture and needed for those under him to grab his vision quickly and assume responsibility for making certain results happen. He needed to paint with a broad brush and have others fill in the pieces. He'd probably never sat down and analyzed his own work style. He definitely expected everyone to move at the same speed he moved and think as he thought. And, of course, they didn't.

His employee was obviously a steady, methodical, process-oriented person who needed someone to show him how the job should be done. He needed the plan clearly laid out and all the details explained. His responsibility would be to do the job right, rather than to make bottom-line results happen.

One person thought about results; the other thought about process. They saw the world through totally different frames of reference. Neither understood how the other thought or operated—each stressed out by the other.

Sound familiar?

It happens all the time whenever people work together. Lots of money and human energy are wasted because people don't understand each other—what they say, what they think, what they mean, or how they feel. The productivity of your people is significantly influenced by their ability to communicate.

Ability to Communicate Influences Productivity

Ralph Waldo Emerson once wrote, "It is a luxury to be understood." Indeed. And it's a luxury that most people don't enjoy enough. Surveys show that a great percentage feel misunderstood by others—especially their managers.

The screenwriter, Mike Nichols once wrote, "You'll never really know what I mean and I'll never know exactly what you mean."

How true!

The miracle of communication is that we communicate as well as we do. Forget for a moment our futile and frustrating attempts to communicate and understand the complexity of our natures. Think about the intricacies of our egos, beliefs, self-images, and backgrounds. Add to this the uniqueness of our experiences, assumptions, and biases, then think about language and cultural differences, regional speech patterns and semantics. You'll marvel that we communicate at all given such complex mechanisms.

One of my favorite writers (as you've obviously figured out by now) is Emerson, who wrote so eloquently in his essay "Experience," "Life is a train of moods like a string of beads, and as we pass through them they prove to be many-colored lenses which paint the world their own hue, and each shows only what lies in its focus."

Considering that of the billions of people on the earth, no one has ever existed who looks or thinks like you or has had the same experiences that you have, the odds against are astronomical that you and I are going to share enough common understanding to see the world in remotely the same way. Each of us looks through lots of filters as we frame our concepts of how things are—heredity, environment, experiences, values, beliefs, and biases. So how are we ever going to have common ground?

You, as a leader, wrestle daily with these complexities of human nature; and they continually influence the productivity of your people. Not only interpersonal communication and understanding, but also departmental or organizational. The composite of your people's communication skills influences the limits of your productivity. In this chapter I'll give you some ideas and suggestions that can help you understand and communicate effectively with your people.

Let's begin with a most obvious and basic assumption: People are different! (Contain yourself! I know that you're not exposed to this incredibly deep level of wisdom all the time; and I can appreciate the adrenaline-pumping experience you've just had as I shared this amazing new discovery with you. But at least just try to control your wild emotions. Okay?)

Think of six people with whom you work. Then analyze their differences—their manners, emotional tone, energy level, speech patterns, views of the world, values, productivity levels, etc. Not exactly all cut out of the same cloth, are they?

In order to make sense out of these complexities, let me

share a model that will help you understand and communicate effectively with people.

People Exhibit Different Behavior Styles

In order to understand your people better—why they think and act as they do—let me present the following model of Behavior Styles.

First, let's think how some people are results-oriented, while others are more task-or process-focused. Like this:

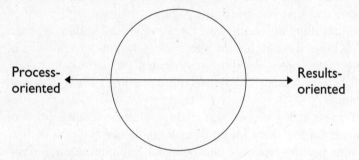

Then let's note that some people are motivated by recognition; others are more interested in security.

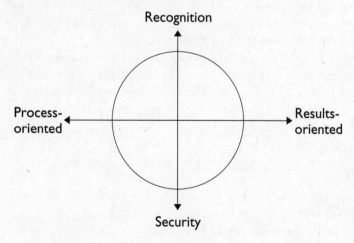

So, let's consider someone who's results-oriented but recognition-motivated; we'll call this person a *Doer*. Someone who's motivated by recognition but more process-focused and not bottom-line-oriented, let's call a *Talker*. A person who's results-oriented but security-motivated we'll call a *Controller*. And a person who's task-or process-oriented and security-motivated, we'll call a *Plodder*.

So, now our model looks like this.

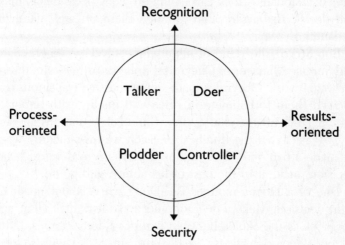

Let's consider each one.

Doers

Doers are bottom-line, get-it-done people. Their need for recognition is that you will recognize them for their achievements, not necessarily like them. They want you to respect them for what they make happen. Because of their need for achievement, they are risk-takers. They *enjoy* taking risks. It gives them the "thrill of the hunt," pumps adrenaline.

Highly energetic, restless, and constantly on the move, they must conquer new worlds, blaze new trails, and see what's on the other side of the mountain. Impatient with the status quo, they exhibit nervous mannerisms—drumming their fingers, moving constantly, and discharging the high energy they have.

Doers enjoy making decisions. They often make quick decisions once they *feel* they have a grasp of the facts. They don't have to have all the facts, just an overall feel for them. Their decisions don't have to always be right; as long as they have a high batting average. It's okay with them to make some bad ones occasionally—they can handle it. They occasionally make bad decisions, but are able to laugh them off and march on undaunted.

Bob Strarr is a friend of mine who retired as General Sales and Service Manager of Chevrolet. Bob was at the helm during the years when Chevrolet made some massive transitions that allowed them to compete in price and quality with imported cars. A Doer off the charts, Bob would laugh, slap his leg, and say, "Wasn't that the dumbest decision we ever made?" when he made a bad one. With that he'd move on to the next major decision, make it to the best of his ability, and go on.

One of a Doer's mottoes is, "Don't worry about making a right decision. Make a decision and make it right!" They view decisions as the choice between two possible outcomes. Often a Doer's decision style is, "Ready, fire, aim . . ." They also focus on the big picture and rely on others to fill in the details. They don't get lost in minutiae or sweat the small stuff.

Doers' greatest fear is the loss of power. Take their decision-making power away from them and you render the coup de grâce to them. Try to control their destiny and you often cause them to bolt and run. Another motto of Doers is, "I don't *get* ulcers. I *give* 'em!"

High energy, color, enthusiasm, charisma—all are Doer qualities. They need to set their own goals and agenda. Manage them too tightly and they'll tell you to take the job and shove it, and move on to one that allows them more latitude.

Since they're high achievers, they also have high ego drive! They want to look good and have people respect them for their achievements. Status is often a high priority—a nice car, large home, the right club.

Doers usually have trophies out for people to see. Just yesterday, I was in the office of a highly effective Doer. Rick Miller is Executive Director of the Boys and Girls Clubs of Metropolitan Phoenix. In his twenty-plus-year tenure he has built this wonderful organization into one with 11,000 kids in its program. Trophies everywhere in his office—pictures of him with Presidents Bush, Reagan, and Carter. Plaques and autographed objects abounded. All of these well-deserved moments came to him as a result of his great works, and they each represented high points of his career. He's obviously proud of these "proofs" of his success, and deservedly so.

Talkers

Talkers are social. They love to visit, socialize with, and be around people. They like parties and other social gatherings. They're easy to approach and get talking. They love stories, jokes, and having the lowdown on others.

Talkers' greatest need is for social approval and their greatest fear is the loss of it. They'll make decisions based on how it's going to make them look to others. They'll be swayed by their need for approval. They view decisions as the choice between what two people want them to do; since they don't like to reject people any more than they like to be rejected, they avoid decisions.

Talkers are usually very popular with others. They're full of life and fun and usually have a joke or story to tell others. For this reason they're often the center of attention wherever groups of people gather. They're the life of the party, often quite charismatic and exciting to be around, never at a loss for words.

Since Talkers' greatest need is for social approval, they often promise more than they'll deliver. They sacrifice back-end delivery for front-end approval. This usually comes back to haunt them. They lose face, which is what they sought to avoid.

They're stressed out with responsibility and accountability for results because that's just not how they think. Details stress them, as do routine, redundant jobs. They must be around people—having constant contact with others.

Talkers are often great trainers or speakers. This gives them lots of applause and approval; as well as a platform to . . . yeah . . . you guessed it . . . talk! Their message is often much better than their practice. They'll have every time-management system made, teach it brilliantly, and never use it themselves.

In the past many sales managers have made the mistake of thinking that because a person liked people, was extroverted, and had a lot of friends that he'd be an effective salesperson. In many cases, they were highly disappointed. The truth is that pure Talkers aren't good salespeople, despite the stereotype, because they can't risk rejection. Their need for social approval prevents them from asking friends or family to buy from them, and from moving people to decisions.

Talkers are often the least effective time managers, often having little or no concept of time or timeliness. Many things are more important—fun and visiting with people, for instance.

Talkers have difficulty working alone. They must have social contact and direction. Isolate them in a work environment and you'll stress them.

Controllers

Controllers are logical, rational, well-organized people. They show high attention to detail. They like numbers, facts, statistics. Their motto is, "A place for everything; everything in its place!" Another motto is, "Ready, ready, ready, aim, aim, aim . . ." Contrast this with a Talker's motto, "Ready . . . hey, where'd I lose the gun?"

Controllers are intellectually driven. For them it's difficult to understand emotional concepts. They just don't think that way. Everything has to have a logical answer. All the numbers have to balance—the debits, credits, and capital always must balance. With their fetish for accuracy, their greatest fear is that of making mistakes. Perfectionistic, they're also often quite critical of things and people who aren't perfect. And since not many of us are perfect (only you and I), they can usually find stuff to criticize in most everyone.

Recently I called on a strong Controller. He seemed cold and indifferent. Showing no emotion, he cut quickly to the chase. No chitchat. It was "What do you have and how much is it?" His demeanor was very removed, distant. His inspection of me bordered on a scowl. These aren't easy people for me to relate to, so I thought to myself, *Hey, man, this guy ain't on the same wavelength with me. I'm wastin' my time!* He gave me virtually no positive responses or reinforcement—like nodding his head, smiling, or displaying any glint of humanness. After he'd asked some very intelligent, logical, penetrating questions about the results of our training, and I had presented proof that we get results, he calmly said he liked it and they were ready to go.

You could have blown me over with a butterfly's wing. I totally misread him.

Controllers evaluate things based on provable results tempered with low risk. Doers ask themselves, "What are the expected results?" Controllers ask, "What are the expected results divided by the risk factors?" They tend to mistrust people who overstate things. They want to know the down side, the possible bad news, what could go wrong. They often don't trust Talkers because they don't give enough attention to details and tend to overpromise and underdeliver. Drop a three-hundred page report on their desk, and it'll only take sixteen seconds for them to discover the typo or mistake on page 128. When this happens, they'll question the validity of the whole report and demand that someone do a report who knows what they're doing.

Perfectionistic, they can also be oppositional in nature. Say the sky is blue and they may disagree and say, "It's not really blue, it's more silver." Or "Can't you be more specific? What percent is blue contrasted with silver?" Not driven by compatibility, if you say, "It's a great day today," They may examine your conclusion, disagree and reply, "I disagree, it's not a good day, the Dow Jones Average is down 6 ⅜ points."

Controllers are great at handling money. They don't make emotional decisions. They're good planners. Every organization needs them to keep the books balanced and relate to their bankers (who love, understand, and trust Controllers).

Plodders

Plodders are steady, dependable, honest, salt-of-the-earth people. Since they're process-or task-focused, they love routine, predictable, consistent jobs. They need sameness and security. They are punctual and timely, conscientious, precise, and trustworthy.

Plodders aren't risk-takers. They don't make decisions easily and have to "sleep on it" before committing to a course of action. Security conscious, they seek to remove or avoid risks. Their greatest fear is the loss of security. They don't usually see the big picture because they focus on the job or process. Not entrepreneurial because that involves risk, they're also not the ones who constantly bombard you with new ideas about how to get more results. Usually they're not creative.

Plodders hang on to old treasured things. They maintain their possessions well. They keep old clothes, knowing they'll come back in style twenty years from now; and look at all the money they'll save. They don't like debt and will often save up and pay cash for something.

I remember several years ago having two employees come into my office, within a few days of each other, telling me about buying new cars. One was a real Talker—earned the highest income of all our people. He asked for an advance on his next paycheck in order to make a down payment on a new Cadillac. He lived high and spent everything he earned.

The other person earned about one-third of the Cadillac-fancier's salary. He told me he had just paid cash for a new

Oldsmobile. If he'd had to go in debt to purchase a car, it would have given him a case of terminal hives.

So much for descriptions of each style. Let's move on to some other concepts about these styles so you can better understand and communicate with your people.

Miscellaneous Concepts

First, let me say that almost no one is a single quadrant style. Most people are combinations of two styles; a few blend three. These people are, as a rule, much more complex. Often their third style is one they've worked to acquire.

When people are combinations of two styles, the styles are often contiguous. Usually one of the styles will be dominant, though.

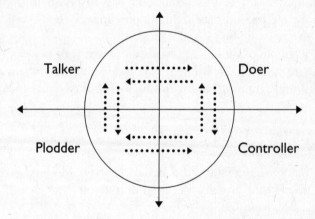

Next, let me emphasize that no style should be considered better than others. We're all different—whatever our style, we have our own unique *strengths* and *weaknesses*.

Also, every organization or team needs a combination of *all* the styles in order to function efficiently. If you had all Doers in an organization, you'd have chaos—butting heads, fighting for turf, and having ego clashes. An organization filled with Controllers would suffer paralysis by analysis—lots of planning, not a lot of execution. One with only Talkers would have constant office parties and lots of fun, but little work would get accomplished. One filled with Plodders would have lots of compliance to rules and regulations but not many new ideas would appear.

Behavior Styles Worksheet

On the following page is a Behavior Styles Worksheet. You may photocopy it and do it on your people . . . and yourself (which, of course, is the perfect style).

Beside the categories are four descriptors. Check the one that most accurately describes the person you're evaluating. At the bottom, circle the style that got the most check marks and underline the one with the second highest number. This will indicate a person's primary and secondary style.

You may ask, "Is this accurate?" My response is that it's probably 80 percent accurate, depending on how well you know the person you're evaluating.

Do a couple of these worksheets on two of your people, then do one on yourself. It will help you understand how you match up with and communicate with others—or miscommunicate.

Insights into This Model

Now that you understand the Behavior Styles Model, here are some points that probably jumped out at you.

1. People think, act, and respond differently.
2. People have different pace, tone, and ways of looking at the world.
3. People's Behavior Styles prepare them for certain jobs, functions, or activities better than others.
4. People naturally assume that others think, feel, and view the world the same way they do.

Behavior Styles Worksheet

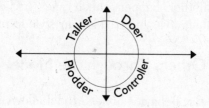

Person's Name _____

Quickly select the description that *best* fits the above-named person.

Personality:	Outgoing ( )	Dominating ( )	Easygoing ( )	No-Nonsense ( )
Environment:	Cluttered/ Pictures ( )	Trophies/ Awards ( )	Keepsakes/ Relics ( )	Order/ Charts ( )
Personal Style:	People-oriented ( )	Results-oriented ( )	Process-oriented ( )	Facts-oriented ( )
Responsiveness:	Friendly/ Affable ( )	Impatient/ Restless ( )	Steady/ Reserved ( )	Cool/ Distant ( )
Listening:	Drifting ( )	Impatient ( )	Willing ( )	Selective ( )
Talks:	About People ( )	About Achievement ( )	About Functions ( )	About Organization ( )
Relations:	Empathizes with others ( )	Commands Others ( )	Accepts Others ( )	Assesses Others ( )
Decisiveness:	Popular/ Emotional ( )	Quick/ Impulsive ( )	Slow/ Studied ( )	Objective/ Fact-Based ( )
Time Usage:	Socializes at expense of time ( )	Always pushed for time ( )	Respects time but not pushed ( )	Values & manages time well ( )
Pace:	Enthusiastic ( )	Fast ( )	Steady ( )	Controlled ( )
Voice:	Emotional/ Animated ( )	Emotional/ Direct ( )	Unemotional/ Low-Keyed ( )	Unemotional/ Reserved ( )
Gestures:	Open ( )	Impatient ( )	Measured ( )	Closed ( )
Dress:	Stylish ( )	Formal ( )	Conforming ( )	Conservative ( )
Manner:	Friendly ( )	Dominating ( )	Accepting ( )	Evaluating ( )
Conversation:	People ( )	Bottom Line ( )	Systems ( )	Facts ( )
	Talker	**Doer**	**Plodder**	**Controller**

5. People will usually communicate with others in a way consistent with their own styles—which is why they often fail to communicate.

6. Rapport with others happens much quicker when we understand their style and change our style to mirror theirs.

Listening to Others Through the Model

Understanding the Behavior Styles Model allows you to listen to people more effectively. It's really a *listening* model; not an analytic one. This model can help you truly listen to and understand what people are saying to you.

It's here that your own style influences communication so powerfully. Generally, if your style is different from another's, you may not really hear him or her because you're speaking two different languages, speaking and listening through different filters.

A Talker miscommunicates with a Controller because a Controller wants facts, figures, and rational information; not emotional, touchy-feely stuff. And vice versa—Controllers seem dull, unemotional, and cold to Talkers. Doers miscommunicate with Plodders because they tend to run over them and move too quickly for them. And, again, vice versa—Plodders tend to move too slowly and drag things out too methodically for Doers.

Well, you get the picture.

Placing Square Pegs in Square Holes

People are often put in job roles that don't suit them. This causes stress and dissatisfaction, on their part and yours.

Recently, I heard a computer expert tell how in ten years no one will be going to offices. They'll all work at home with computers hooked to a modem into their office. He was convinced that what he predicted would happen. All you had to do was listen to the dryness of his presentation and see his obvious enthrallment with technology to understand why he'd make such a statement. To him (a Controller/Plodder no doubt) this was very logical.

Of course, there was some validity to what he said. Certain types of people (his style) would eat that up. Others (Talkers) would be driven up the wall if they were at a computer terminal all day, with no social contact, and expected to get everything done.

Study Behavior Styles and you will find all kinds of holes in the man's prediction.

I also get quite a laugh out of technicians who design elaborate software systems for salespeople to use, and then find that these highly motivated Doers want to spend their time in front of clients or customers, not filling in all the reports that have been conjured up for them.

Now, before you get offended at what I'm saying, let me tell you that I'm simply expressing the bias of my own style. So, you can see how we all fail to communicate.

How to Improve Communication

To improve communication, first understand the concept of Behavior Styles, then observe people's mannerisms, speed, tone, and what they want to talk about. As you observe people, you can blend your style with theirs. Since you know how they feel and respond; adopt their pace, tone, and attitude. See the world through their eyes. Match their tone, tempo, energy, and volume.

Focus constantly on this for twenty-one days, and then you'll begin to do it automatically. Soon you'll get so good that you'll just naturally do this—as an unconscious behavior.

This subject always brings up an event that happened several years ago when we brought our *Integrity Selling*® program to around nine-hundred Chevrolet dealers. Mike Esterday, one of our trainers, was conducting three-day certification seminars for dealership managers, who would in turn conduct a course at their dealerships.

Mike was explaining the Behavior Styles concept—how their salespeople should identify a customer's style and then match it. After explaining it, Mike looked at a manager named Buck and could tell that no lights were on behind his eyes. Buck obviously hadn't grabbed the point. So Mike explained it one more time. Still no lights. So, he did it a third time. About halfway through the third explanation, Buck's eyes lit up. He'd gotten it. Raising his hand, he said, "Oh, Mike, I'm just understanding what you're tryin' to tell us. You're saying that when a customer comes in, we should approach 'em in neutral, identify their style, and then change our style . . . like one of those animals that changes color to fit their surroundings . . . like one of those *charlatans*!"

Now, we're not sure, but we thought this might qualify as one of those, what do you call them . . . oh yeah . . . Freudian slips!

Summing Up

Understanding this Behavior Styles Model allows you to understand that different people see things different ways. Unless you understand how they think, feel, and act, you'll miscommunicate.

Most of us unconsciously think that ours is the normal style. So, it's not easy to understand why others don't see the world the same way we do.

Understanding Behavior Styles and blending our style to match others' styles reduces stress in communication and helps us achieve rapport and emotionally bond with people. It also helps us understand how people go about their business naturally, so we know what jobs to expect, or not expect, people to do.

As a manager, you can see that you'll stress people if you try to force them into jobs that don't suit their natural styles. Then the harder you push or demand results, the more stress there will be. Finally, built-up stress will cause burnout, blowout, or walkout.

This week, fill in several Behavior Styles Worksheets on people with whom you work. Fill one in on yourself. See if you can discover why you either do or don't communicate well with those people.

This model can give you a simple, yet highly effective, framework for getting more done through people.

How to Gain the Most from This Chapter

So much of your success as a leader depends on your ability to communicate with people—to listen, hear, speak, understand. Managers or leaders often expect everyone to communicate the way they do, but people hear through their own filters.

To benefit the most from this session, practice these ideas.

1. Digest the Behavior Styles Model. Spend a week reading and practicing the ideas in this chapter.
2. Photocopy the worksheet page and fill it in on two people with whom you communicate well and two with whom you find it difficult to communicate.
3. Do a sheet on yourself and see how your style might conflict or fit well with the people you profiled.
4. Read and meditate on the six insights into this model. Apply what you read to people you know.
5. Use the model to listen and let it help you hear what different people are telling you.

People can be taught to solve problems and make decisions instead of constantly bugging you with all kinds of little, nitty questions or concerns!

8. "Hey, Boss, I Have This Problem I Want to Dump on Your Shoulders!"

The message from the moon is that no problem need any longer be considered insolvable.

—NORMAN COUSINS

A leader teaches others to lead themselves—to solve their own problems, make their own decisions, act with strong positive values and produce agreed-upon results with their own given resources.

I'm not at all advocating that you turn all your decisions over to your people. Of course, you'll always make the major decisions, but the more decisions you can empower your people to make, the more broad-based a leader you'll become. You'll be freed up to do what leaders do—set the vision for your organization's future by selecting competent people, motivating and inspiring them.

How much of your time is spent solving problems that people should be solving themselves?

If you're average, a great deal of your own productive time is taken up by your own people asking you to solve problems that they're paid to solve and make decisions that they're employed to make.

Get-stuff-done leaders refuse to solve other people's problems; rather they train them how to do it and then empower them to do it. Contrast this with codependent people who assume that their role in life is to shoulder the world's problems and take responsibility that others should take. Consequently, they get mired down in the minutiae that eventually engulfs and often immobilizes them.

So, not only is their own leadership effectiveness drained off by others, but they fail to build problem-solving and decision-making skills in their people. And since many people are thrilled to let someone else make their decisions, they shuffle all they can to other people.

Reflecting on human nature, Thomas Edison once remarked, "There is no expedient to which a man will not go to avoid the real labor of thinking."

Cynical? Well, maybe a bit, but observe human nature and you'll quickly see that many people will leave their thinking up to another person.

Leaders leverage their own time and talents by teaching their people to make most of their decisions and solve their own problems. Usually, the more they can do this, the more they get done through people.

How to Empower People to Solve Problems and Make Decisions

In order to empower people to solve more of their own problems and make their own decisions, you'll need to do the following.

1. Teach them logical problem-solving and decision-making processes.
2. Refuse to allow them to shift responsibility to your shoulders.
3. Coach them on how to apply the processes.

In this chapter I'll share two formulas that you can teach your people. I'll also share some ideas that can help you help your people develop appropriate behaviors. This will save huge amounts of your time and energy and increase your people's productivity.

How to Solve Problems with Customers

The following is a simple and logical customer-service problem-solving formula that many of our course participants have used. It's easy to understand and implement. Your people don't have to be Mensa members to understand and do it.

Copy this formula and give it out to your people. Whenever someone comes to you and asks you what you would do about a given situation, pull out a sheet, hand it to them, and respond, "I haven't the slightest idea. Why don't you go work this problem-solving formula and tell me what's the best way to solve it?"

Customer-Service Problem-Solving Formula

1. *Understand* the problem.
   a. Get all the facts.
   b. Listen nondefensively to customers.
   c. Repeat the problem as you understood it.

2. *Identify* the cause.
   a. Find out what happened.
   b. Find out what should have happened.
   c. Find out what went wrong.

3. *Discuss* possible solutions with customers.
   a. Suggest options.
   b. Ask for other people's ideas.
   c. Agree on the best course of action.

4. *Solve* the problem.
   a. Remove the cause, or

b. Take corrective action.
c. Ask the people involved if they are satisfied with the resolution.

This simple customer-service problem-solving formula helps your people set emotions aside and logically reach a satisfactory resolution.

Give this formula to anyone who comes to you with customer-service issues. Tell them they're better prepared to solve the problem than you are. Give them the formula, ask them to work through it; arrive at what they think is the best solution; and then come back to you to review their analysis.

This assignment may take ten minutes or ten days, but if you hold their feet to the fire and get them thinking and working through the formula, you'll equip them to work through many problems for which they don't need your help. Even for problems that may require your input, have them go through the formula analysis anyway before coming to you. Ask them:

1. What's the problem?
2. What's the cause?
3. What's your recommendation for a solution?
4. Will the customer be happy with this solution?

After you've reviewed their problem analysis, you can approve their corrective action or suggest changes. Whichever, you've bolstered the person and kept the problem-solving responsibility on his/her shoulders.

Now, let's consider the logic of this formula. First, customer-service problems usually involve emotions, and this can block logic and good judgment. Egos get involved. Turf must be protected. Battle lines are drawn. Using nonjudgmental listening, this formula allows your people to defuse customers' emotions by getting them talking.

It's here that your people's attitudes strongly influence the outcome. Their attitudes should be, "Let's understand the problem and work toward a solution that pleases you. Let me make sure I understand what caused the problem, discuss possible solutions, and then solve the problem."

When your people demonstrate genuine care and concern, they will resolve problems and strengthen customer relations.

Now, I realize that your people have other problems that don't involve internal or external customers. So let me share with you another simple problem-solving formula that works well when encountering process or functional problems.

A General Problem-Solving Formula

Below is a general problem-solving formula for you to teach your people when they're dealing with more process-oriented or functional problems.

A General Problem-Solving Formula

1. Define the problem.
   a. What was the desired outcome?
   b. What was the actual outcome?
   c. What was the deviation or difference?

2. Identify the cause of the problem.
   a. What went wrong?
   b. Why did it go wrong?
   c. What unforeseen factors entered in?

3. Write down possible solutions.
   a. List everything you can think of that will remove the cause or correct the deviation.
   b. Research and seek the advice of others.
   c. Analyze each possible solution as to its ability to eliminate the cause or deviation.

4. Solve the problem.
   a. Seek to eliminate the cause of the problem.

b. Choose best solutions and prioritize them.
c. Begin doing them one at a time.

What Is a Problem?

A problem is the difference between what should have happened and what actually happened.

The first step in problem solving is to identify and understand the problem. Sounds simple, doesn't it? But, as I've said before, people who experience problems often move out of a logical mode into an emotional one.

Edward Hodnett once wrote, "A good problem statement often includes: (a) What is known, (b) What is unknown, and (c) What is sought."

Akin to this, it was Charles Kettering, early genius of design and engineering at General Motors, who advised, "A problem well stated is a problem half-solved." A problem understood and well-defined in writing gets your people a long way down the road to solving it.

Often people seek solutions before the true problem is known. Which reminds me of a statement I once read from the pen of the famous G. K. Chesterton, "It isn't that they can't see the solution. It is that they can't see the problem."

Define the Problem

Defining the problem gets your people to focus on solving the problem rather than being overwhelmed with the problem's repercussions. Often, the anxiety that we allow problems to cause within us blocks our ability to think. You've seen it many times. One of your people comes in and frantically tells you, "We can't get orders out and the sales department is already getting calls from angry customers, and the people who fill orders don't have anything to do and everyone is screaming at everyone else . . ."

You've seen similar situations, haven't you? People focusing on the anxiety that the problem has created instead of defining the problem, identifying the cause, and taking corrective action.

Identify the Cause

The obvious problem was that orders weren't being processed. So the first question is, "Why aren't they getting out? What's causing the problem?"

Theoretically, every problem has a cause and when the cause is identified and corrected, the problem gets solved. This is a bit simplistic, but the theory can at least keep people on a logical track.

There are many causes of problems. They can be functional—the computer malfunctioned. They can be operational—the assembly line isn't properly designed. They can be personal—two people are having personal conflicts.

In order to solve the problems, the cause of them has to be identified. You can help your people identify the cause by getting them doing these three actions. Identify:

1. What went wrong?
2. Why did it go wrong?
3. What unforeseen factors entered in?

Asking and writing down answers to these questions can help them get at the root cause of the problem. It's here that your people often stop and come to you for you to do their problem analysis for them. They ask, "We've got this problem. What do you want us to do about it?"

Very often you're drawn into allowing them to shift the responsibility to you. I know that sometimes you do need to handle it; but I'll guess that most often you don't need to solve it—your people are quite capable of doing that. They often just don't want to take the responsibility.

To condition your people to become problem solvers, you might encourage a dialogue like this:

ASSOCIATE: "Hey, boss, I've got this problem. What do you think I ought to do about it?"

YOU: "I haven't the slightest idea. What do *you* think *you* should do?"

ASSOCIATE: "Well, I was hoping you could, you know, sorta, help me solve it!"

YOU: "Tell you what. You take this problem-solving formula and work through it. Let me take a few minutes and explain it to you. (Give person a sheet with formula printed on it and explain it.)

"Go work through it and then come back to me with your ideas. We'll sit down and go over what you think the problem is, what caused it, and how you think we can solve it."

ASSOCIATE: "You mean you aren't going to continue to be co-dependent and allow me to dump all this stuff on you that I don't want to take responsibility for?"

YOU: "Yeah, something like that! Bye for now . . ."

Well, maybe I'm exaggerating a bit.

Empowering Your People

Enough has been written about empowering people to educate everyone from here to Pluto. A lot of it is good advice, but much is wasted and empty. Here are some factors that influence the empowerment of people.

1. They must understand the objectives.
2. They must understand the rules, values, and guidelines to stay within.

3. They must take responsibility.

4. You must give them freedom within certain limits to solve problems and make decisions.

5. You must not beat them up when they make a wrong decision. It must become a learning experience.

6. You must encourage your people to own each problem they encounter.

7. You have to train and build your people, and then trust them to do the right things.

8. You must celebrate victories and growth.

9. You must get cross-functional teams working on problems and objectives.

10. You must help each person see how his or her role fits into the overall success of your organization.

This is a new role for many managers. In the traditional, top to bottom, hierarchical type of management structure, managers made decisions and passed them down to subordinates. That's not an efficient organizational structure.

A major problem in today's business environment stems from restructuring. The trauma, paranoia, and fear that result from layoffs block people's willingness to take corrective actions that place them in jeopardy. So, many people opt to play it safe and not stick their necks out.

People Assume Responsibility When Basic Needs Are Met

We can pontificate and blow smoke about empowerment until it snows in Phoenix, but people aren't going to stick their necks out and take responsibility until certain needs are met and their culture permits it. Before people assume responsibility for making decisions and solving problems, they must have:

1. A clear understanding of your organization's vision—what you will look like in the future.
2. A clear understanding of their job roles and how they fit into that vision.
3. Training to look for and solve problems.
4. Encouragement to be creative and innovative.
5. Acknowledgment of and reward for their successes, even attempts.
6. A sense that they are genuinely valued and given autonomy.

Now, you may say that you live in the real world and you have people who resist change like politicians resist truth. You've got "goof-offs" who, if you gave them responsibility for results, would hide in the nearest broom closet.

Of course, there are people like that, people who are process-oriented and will never be creative, innovative, or entrepreneurial.

A few people resist change so much that you'll never convert them; at least it would take too much time and effort to try to change them. So, you carefully look for the right qualities in new people.

An Organization That Thrives on Empowerment

One of our clients and business partners is the Ritz-Carlton Hotel. A recent winner of the Malcolm Baldridge Quality Award, they walk their talk when it comes to empowering their people.

About twenty people are interviewed in order to hire one new employee. They look, not for experience, but for friendliness and natural human-relations skills. In extensive training, they teach people the culture of Ritz-Carlton. They learn about the whole operation, front to back. They cross-train in all departments.

Each employee carries a Credo Card inscribed with the following:

> The Ritz-Carlton Hotel is a place where the genuine care and comfort of our guests is our highest mission.
>
> We pledge to provide the finest personal service and facilities for our guests who will always enjoy a warm, relaxed yet refined ambiance.
>
> The Ritz-Carlton experience enlivens the senses, instills well-being, and fulfills even the unexpressed wishes and needs of our guests.

Their battle cry is "We are Ladies and Gentlemen Serving Ladies and Gentlemen!"

They identify three steps of service:

1. A warm and sincere greeting. Use the guests' names, if and when possible.
2. Anticipation of and compliance with guests' needs.
3. Fond farewell. Give them a warm good-bye and use their names, if and when possible.

On the inside of the fold-over card, they outline twenty "Ritz-Carlton Basics" to be practiced by all their people on a daily basis.

Each employee carries a Credo Card at all times. They focus on one of the twenty basics each day. Every employee of every hotel around the world focuses on that same basic the same day. Talk about synergy. Can you imagine the energy and power generated by every employee around the world focusing on the same action each day?

Because Ritz-Carlton selects the right kind of people, trains them, communicates their vision and beliefs and core values, their employees *look* for creative ways to solve problems and satisfy guests.

One evening one of our clients checked into the Ritz-Carlton in Phoenix, where we hold seminars. Her luggage had been lost and it was about 10 P.M. when she arrived. The desk clerk told her that they kept some clothes available for emergencies like this. Surprised, she thanked the person and said she was sure that the airline would find her luggage by morning.

Are you ready for this? About ten minutes after settling in her room, another person called and said he had heard about her problem, that his wife was about her size, and that she was bringing three outfits down so she could select one to wear the next day.

How about that for customer service?

Taking Ownership of Problems

One of the points on the Credo Card is, "Any employee who receives a guest complaint 'owns' the complaint." Everyone is trained to take ownership of problems as they spot them. Each one is empowered to solve a problem up to $2,000 without asking anyone.

This practice shifts tremendous decision-making powers to all employees. Obviously they have to be trained to accept this level of responsibility. Not just trained to handle problems, but also trained emotionally to accept responsibility and move ahead confidently with corrective actions. Of course, this practice influences the type of people they hire.

It also makes a powerful statement of confidence in their people. It says, "We trust you to use your best judgment and take care of problems as they occur."

When you're confident in your people's ability to act responsibly, they'll work hard to live up to your faith in them.

To make the Ritz-Carlton model work, employees not only have to be trained, but there must be an atmosphere that encourages initiative and creativity. The Ritz-Carlton employees actively seek innovative ways to give extra service or make guests happy. But they also know they'll not get beaten up if they make a bad decision—it'll be a learning experience.

Innovation can't flourish if people fear punishment when things don't work out exactly right. This doesn't mean that you should give people a free rein to do whatever they want. There must be boundaries, of course.

Releasing Control

Empowering people means, in a sense, relinquishing control. And many managers equate having control with how valuable they are to their organizations.

This is bad thinking.

Often, keeping control limits productivity. If you're a person who micromanages, you'll just naturally limit your productivity. There aren't enough hours in the day for you to be involved in every decision your people have to make.

Add this to the fact that you'll never build strong self-motivated people if you micromanage them. This is true for two reasons. First, you'll kill any creative, entrepreneurial spirit in them with oversupervision and second-guessing. Second, you'll not attract and keep people who are geared to making decisions, solving problems, and exercising personal initiative and achievement drive. Highly motivated, get-it-done people want to know your objectives and expectations, the boundaries and parameters in which to operate; and then have the freedom and latitude with which to go make it happen.

Control is a paradoxical, often illusional thing. Often when you think you have it, you don't. Often when you think having it is important to keep your job, you lose your position by hanging on to it. Control may give people a sense of power, but the more they rely on it, the more their chances of losing power increase. The person who has real power is the one who can select good people, train them, and give them the latitude to work and get results.

Decision Making

Decision making is what course of action to take after a problem has been solved.

Napoleon Hill, author of the classic *Think and Grow Rich* wrote, after studying the lives of five hundred of the most successful people of his era, that each one had the ability to sort out the facts and, after understanding them, make a quick decision, and stick with it.

"*All* of these people had this unique trait," he underscored.

They were successful, he emphasized, not because all their decisions were good ones; but because they acted on their best judgment and then went on to take action. Of course, they made bad decisions. We all do.

Highly effective people can size up situations, facts, and data, then decide. Mistakes will be made, but they are more than offset by the benefits of conscientiousness, decisiveness, and action. This spawned a saying that I've mentioned before, "Don't worry about making a right decision; make a decision and make it right!"

Many people spend years in flux, collecting data, attempting to make a good decision but afraid of making a bad one.

There are many decision-making models. For 90 percent of decisions, the old Ben Franklin Model can prove very helpful:

1. At the top of a page define the course of action that you think would be the best decision.
2. Draw a vertical line dividing the sheet in half.
3. On one side list all the reasons for taking the action; and on the other side list all the dangers or reasons not to take the action.
4. Compare the pros and cons, choose one, and move on or initiate the course of action.

Give this simple decision-making model to your people. Obviously, for complicated, high-risk decisions, more thought and analysis needs to be given to it. But for 90 percent of their decisions, this method will work.

Summing Up

One way to get more done through people is to empower them to solve problems and make decisions.

Probably a great deal of your time is consumed by people who want you to solve their problems and make their decisions for them.

It all begins with people who will take initiative and responsibility and then setting the boundaries and parameters in which they can make decisions. Then they need to be trained in problem solving and decision making. Once trained they need to be empowered to take action, use their best judgment, and move through the problems and decisions they encounter.

In this chapter I have given you two problem-solving models. One for a customer-service problem; one for a generic problem. I have given you permission to duplicate these models to give to your people and teach them how to use them.

You'll find that through practice and reinforcement they'll gradually grow in their ability to solve problems and make decisions. You'll discover that your people can use these simple models for around 90 percent of their decisions and problems.

Training and empowering your people to use these models will not only save your valuable time and energy, but it will help you get more done through your people, which will greatly increase your value to your organization.

Oh, yes, have you discovered that "something else" that I mentioned in earlier chapters? At this point in your reading, what do you think it is?

Already, it has been suggested to you several times and in several ways.

How to Gain the Most from This Chapter

As you're discovering, when you focus on one chapter for a week, absorb it, and pick out specific actions to take, you'll benefit. It's when you only read the chapter and go on to the next one that few or no results occur.

So to benefit the most this week, try these actions.

1. Photocopy the two problem-solving formulas.
2. Whenever an associate comes to you with a problem, hand a sheet to him and ask him to go work through the formula.
3. Get back with the person, review his analysis and coach him as needed.

Do this continually and you'll develop your people to solve many problems that they heretofore brought to you.

People have a built-in Creative Mechanism that works to convert their dominant thoughts, whether they be negative or positive, into realities!

9. "Let's Find a Way to Make It Work."

Thought makes the whole dignity of man; therefore endeavor to think well, that is the only morality.

—PASCAL

Each of your people thinks in terms of either possibilities or limitations. However they think, they've probably had that pattern for a long time, maybe all their lives. These attitudes or thinking patterns continue unconsciously.

Their thinking patterns have a powerful and profound influence on their performance. Their productivity, whether they sell, manufacture, do data entry or customer service, is inextricably tied to their pattern of thinking, their attitudes.

In this chapter, I'll give you a simple process that you can do with your people that will dramatically expand their thinking and thus increase their productivity.

Your people reveal their thinking patterns with responses like these.

"We've never done it that way before."

"We tried that once and it didn't work."

"I don't think that will work!"

"Let me give it a try!"

"What do we need to make happen?"

"Let's find a way to make it work!"

Some people's attitudes are open, creative, and exploring. Others are closed, rigid, and inflexible.

You already know that, don't you?

You've also noticed a correlation between the way your people think and the kind of jobs they do. You have people who are process-focused and who have to do it exactly the same way without deviation, and some who shoot from the hip and operate out of a very loose structure. You have people who are creative thinkers, constantly looking for ways to get more done and improve your processes, and others who have absolutely no creativity or originality.

You probably have used good judgment and have your people placed in job roles that complement their styles or thinking patterns. I just suspect that you, like most of us who manage or lead, have a number of people whom you'd like to be more creative, innovative, and energetic in figuring out new and better ways to get more done.

People Must Think Differently to Produce More

Before people can become more productive, they'll probably have to learn to think differently. They are where they are because of their accepted habits of thinking. Do they think in terms of new possibilities or in terms of limitations? Are they constantly thinking about how they might do their jobs better, or are they constantly thinking about just doing their jobs? Do they see solutions or do they just myopically see problems?

As I've said, people produce consistent with what they imagine themselves producing. In order to change their outcomes or results, you'll first have to help them change the way they think.

But before I get into ways to help your people become more creative, possibility-oriented thinkers, let me share a basic concept with you.

Every Person Has a Built-in Creative Mechanism

In the years I worked with Dr. Maxwell Maltz, author of the great work *Psycho-Cybernetics*, I learned a great deal about what he called our Creative Mechanism.

In his excellent book, he writes this about this piece of machinery that we each have. "Every living thing has a built-in guidance system or goal-striving device put there by its Creator to help it achieve its goal . . ." he wrote.

This Creative Mechanism, our brain, operates to help us reach goals that are important to us and ones we "believe" possible. The key is that we must believe our goals are possible in order to trigger this mechanism. Otherwise, it lies dormant and inoperative.

What this means is that *thought* and *belief* trigger this powerful mechanism. But not just thought; it's possibility thinking—thought that's accompanied by a belief that what we think about is possible.

This mechanism, when directed toward achievable goals, explains every new discovery, invention, and advancement. Its use brought us electric lights. Benjamin Franklin knew that electricity caused light. He witnessed it when lightning bolts cracked through the sky. He even invented an electric generator, but he could not figure out a way to create sustained light from the generator.

But one hundred years later, Thomas Edison used the same Creative Mechanism in his head and finally created sustained light from electricity. Both used the same process and equipment—their imaginations and creativity, applied toward a target they believed it possible to hit.

A Goal-Seeking Mechanism

The same mechanism is used very differently by weekend golf-
ers as well as greats like Arnold Palmer and Jack Nicklaus. The
weekender steps up to the tee box, hopes his ball doesn't go
into the water; thereby visualizing a negative goal, or thinking
about what he doesn't want to happen. And, of course, his
Goal-Seeking Mechanism silently carries out its programming
and causes certain muscles to react in such a way that sends
the ball into the water or to the spot that was visualized as
where the golfer didn't want it to go.

Jack Nicklaus steps up to the tee box, takes a moment to
visualize where he wants the ball to go, then swings, and his
Goal-Seeking Mechanism silently carries out its programming
and causes certain muscles to react in a way that sends the ball
to the exact spot that was visualized as where he wanted it to
go.

The same thing happened in both cases. The difference,
among other things, was the programming of their inner Mechanism.

Every action, habit, or behavior is a result of your Goal-
Seeking Mechanism. You may not think of it like this, but it's
true. Even the most mundane or routine activity is the result
of its use. You brush your teeth in the morning because your
Mechanism gave a silent command to do it and so your muscles
automatically responded appropriately.

You drive to work each day and get there because your
Goal-Seeking Mechanism was aimed at a target, and it silently
and unconsciously steered you through all the stops and turns
to get you there. You identified a goal and knew it was possible.

Your people all operate the same way in their work activities.
They visualize targets (processes or results) and their Automatic
Mechanism steers them to the result. When they don't think
the goal is within their possibilities, they either don't try or they
step on land mines and block their advancement. When they

focus on the roadblocks, they get clogged up in them. When they focus on a positive result, they move to that.

How Your People Are Stressed

Your people can become highly stressed when you set goals for them, or encourage them to set goals, that they don't believe are possible.

They'll also experience "cognitive dissonance." Dr. Leon Festinger of Stanford University coined the term to mean mental conflicts. Cognitive dissonance, or having mental conflicts, happens whenever people are told to do something or reach goals that they don't think are possible for them to reach.

Mental conflicts cause stress. The more you press your people to perform in ways that they don't think are possible, the more stressed they'll be. And the more stressed they are, the less able they'll be to perform on a higher level—a fact of human nature, unfortunately, that many managers don't understand. When people's productivity begins to drop and stress occurs, many managers simply do what they believe works— they put more pressure on people to produce. Then they wonder why they have high turnover and low-job or -sales performance.

Managers' or Leaders' Role of Building People

Understanding that people can't be driven, only led, brings us to a very important point: Managers and leaders must help people expand their inner beliefs about what's possible for them to achieve. Your role is to help them expand their mental areas of the possible.

Remember, people will exert little or no effort toward goals or levels of performance that they don't view to be within their possibilities. This explains why some people plateau, never seeming to achieve the level of productivity that you think they're capable of.

In the language of a few chapters ago, unless you help people grow in the "I Am" dimension, you will not see significant increases in their productivity. This one statement may very well be the summation of everything I've learned about helping people become more productive.

Your People's View of Their Possibilities Is in Their "I Am" Dimension

Your people's view of their possibilities resides in their "I Am" dimension, near the core of their being. Their level of productivity is inextricably tied to "who" they perceive themselves to be in their "I Am."

It all operates on the unconscious level, so none of us can tell you what's going on in that part of us. It's beyond our conscious knowledge. But it's there, nonetheless, and powerfully influencing all our actions, feelings, behaviors, and abilities.

Well, okay, I've attempted to say this powerful truth several ways to challenge your thinking. So, now that you understand it, let's move on to what actions you can take to help your people develop larger views of their possibilities.

Increasing Possibility Thinking

Dr. Robert Schuller coined the phrase "Possibility Thinking" to mean thinking in terms of positive outcomes rather than negative ones. It's consciously holding thoughts of what could happen that's *good* rather than holding thoughts of what could possibly happen that's *bad*.

Since our Goal-Seeking Mechanism silently steers us toward our dominant thoughts and beliefs, Possibility Thinking is a proactive way to positively influence future events.

Far from a Pollyanna, ivory-towered concept, Possibility

Thinking takes advantage of a great law of the mind—*we become what we think about.*

So, you can see that by consciously selecting what we think about, we can *indirectly* choose positive results by *directly* choosing the thoughts we think.

Now, I realize that you'll encounter skeptics to this approach. You'll hear people who don't buy this philosophy, say such things as, "This isn't logical or realistic." These responses are often just excuses to stay where they are, to resist change, to not run risks or advance.

I'm not at all advocating "wishful thinking" or "sit-on-your-duff and daydream" kind of actions. Possibility Thinking is creative planning and then hard work. It's looking into the future at what great things that can happen, committing to those goals, laying out plans for achievement, and then going to work. This is nothing akin to fantasy. Rather, it's exactly what all trailblazing, successful leaders do.

Possibility Thinking Formula

Below is a formula for Possibility Thinking. It's a process that you probably do unconsciously. When you get your people doing it consciously until they develop unconscious behaviors, you'll see some dramatic increases in their initiative, creativity, and results.

Possibility Thinking Formula

1. Whenever you encounter a problem, situation, or decision, ask yourself, "What is the best possible outcome to the problem, situation, or decision?"

2. Then ask, "Suppose this outcome did happen, how would I feel?"

3. Then ask, "What are the chances of this positive outcome actually happening?"

4. And, finally, ask yourself, "What can I do to make sure this positive outcome actually happens?"

Take out a sheet of paper and select one problem, situation, or decision that you're struggling with now and go through the four-step formula.

Don't get lazy on me. Get a piece of paper and do it. It won't work as well if you try to do it in your head.

The Formula Focuses Your Powerful Goal-Seeking Mechanism

This simple formula focuses your powerful Goal-Seeking Mechanism on a specific target. It moves you through all the clutter and the potholes that draw your focus away from what is important, causing you to spend too much mental energy on brushfires.

I've noticed that highly successful people tend to have common traits. They can cut through the clutter and focus on the positive objective. But many managers (at least in my observation) get so embroiled in the everyday minutiae and "play-not-to-lose" activities that their eyes are largely drawn away from the major objective. They do a great job of housekeeping but don't look for ways to build bigger houses or make their present ones more efficient.

In fact, I've noticed that highly successful leaders even show what appear to be significant blind spots—they ignore nitty, nagging disturbances, delegate those, and subordinate them to the more important vision of reaching specific goals.

As I mentioned before a number of years ago, I had the privilege of working closely for six months with W. Clement Stone. Mr. Stone, a very colorful self-made mega-millionaire, was a true visionary. He had the ability to think both in the micro and macro—he could see the big overall picture yet had an incredible grasp of the facts and basic things that made his organizations run.

I worked with him as a consultant in 1980. His insurance company had an after-tax profit of $90 million, and they were getting ready for major expansion. Here he was in his eighties about to accelerate his company's growth more than ever before. In a few years his organization would purchase numerous others and quadruple its earnings.

He had incredible energy and enthusiasm. Up each morning at a very early hour, he would slowly groom and dress himself, spending at least thirty minutes in quiet "thinking and planning" time. He would review his goals and visualize their fulfillment. He credited much of his success to this habit.

In this daily "thinking and planning time" he cut out everything (distractions, clutter, minor roadblocks), and indulged his mind with the rewards and gratifications of reaching his goals.

Focusing on his goals moved him beyond the problems and difficulties that others get mired in. Over and over he said, "Every problem has a logical solution." He saw problems simply as things to be solved in order to reach a goal.

A friend swears this story about the legendary Vince Lombardi is true. Remember the "Ice Bowl" game between Green Bay and Dallas in 1967? Near the end of the game Green Bay was down on Dallas's one-yard line, having been stymied three times by Dallas's great line anchored by all-pros Bob Lilly and Jethro Pugh. Before the fourth down and last play of the game, Bart Starr called time out and trotted over to the sideline and asked Lombardi, "What do I do, Coach?"

Lombardi screamed into Starr's face, "Score, dammit!" and turned away, leaving the great quarterback alone with the decision.

The goal was clearly communicated. Bart Starr, on his way back to the huddle suddenly pictured a play that they had not run all year—a quarterback sneak. The rest is history—he took the ball and rode on Jerry Kramer's back into the end zone to win the game in the last seconds.

What a great example of a leader focusing on the goal rather than on the obstacles or even the strategy of reaching the goal. Also, an excellent demonstration of the power of Bart Starr's

Goal-Seeking Mechanism at work. The goal was clearly communicated, he was left to come up with a solution, and his powerful Mechanism sent its answer to his conscious mind.

Focus on the goal and the means of attainment will be discovered and revealed by your unconscious, creative, Goal-Seeking Mechanism.

Possibility thinking triggers this powerful Mechanism.

Your Goal-Seeking Mechanism Is Programmed and Triggered by Mental Pictures

Undoubtedly, when Vince Lombardi yelled, "Score, dammit," to Bart Starr, it triggered a mental picture of his team crossing the goal line. W. Clement Stone well understood how his mental pictures helped program his Goal-Seeking Mechanism. He learned, in a relaxed way, to picture and enjoy the end result—the achievement of his goals. He acknowledged that his mental picturing of what he wanted to achieve was a major contribution to his high level of success.

Mental Pictures Reach Our Emotions

Mental pictures bypass our logical minds and touch our emotions—our drives, our needs for gratification and rewards.

Mental picturing helped a young man in one of my classes do something that has not been equaled since.

Ove Johansson came from Sweden to the United States to play soccer for a college in West Virginia. While working in Texas one summer, he helped organize a youth soccer league for the city of Irving. He soon met and married his wife, April, a student at Abilene Christian University, and he transferred there.

Late one November he attended a football game—his first. As a friend was explaining the game, he explained that a field goal was where you kicked the ball through the uprights and got three points. Ove nodded and asked an obvious question, "Well, why don't they kick the ball more?"

His friend explained that in college football not many people could kick over thirty-five yards.

Not understanding the limitation, Ove said, "Oh, I could kick it much farther than that!"

His friend responded, "Then why don't you?"

To which Ove said, "Okay, I will!"

Without broadcasting it, he set a goal in his head to kick a football farther than anyone had ever done before—and to do it in one year. To this day, he still doesn't know why he set that goal or why he even believed he could accomplish it.

In January of the next year, he started practicing each afternoon in the cold west Texas weather. At first the ball didn't exactly cooperate because it wasn't the right shape—it wasn't round like a soccer ball. But he kept after it until he developed more accuracy.

Each afternoon he'd go to a practice field and begin kicking. At first he'd kick from the point where the end zone and sideline intersect. Visualize the narrowness of this angle. Then he'd move the ball back to the ten yard line and sideline and kick.

Gradually he'd move the ball farther and farther back—widening the window about the goalposts. Then he'd move the ball in to the hash marks, then to the center of the field. From there he had what seemed to him an incredibly large opening above the goalposts—which he later said, "made it look like I had the whole world to kick through!"

He played another interesting mental game. Before each kick he'd stand behind the ball and visualize two things:

1. his form in approaching the ball and
2. the ball going perfectly between the uprights.

After visualizing what he wanted to happen, he'd kick—forgetting form, just doing it the way it felt most natural. Regardless of where it landed, he'd mentally correct his kick. He'd visualize it going where he wanted it to go instead of where it had gone.

When he picked the ball up, regardless of where it was, he'd stop, look back at the kicking tee, and visualize himself kicking the ball. He'd mentally review his approach and form in detail. He'd "see" the ball leaving the tee and going perfectly between the goalposts. Then he'd tee the ball up, and begin the process again—for two to three hours each afternoon.

"Didn't that get boring?" I asked him.

"Never," he responded. "It was so exciting—I enjoyed hundreds of successes each afternoon!"

He progressed steadily and by the middle of the summer he was banging fifty- to sixty-yard field goals with ease. A young man who played tight end for Abilene Christian saw him and was aghast.

Approaching Ove, he asked, "Do you know what you're doing?"

"Ya," Ove replied.

"Why, you're . . . you're kicking close to the world record!"

"Ya," Ove replied.

"How far can you kick?" the young man asked.

"Oh, sixty, seventy yards," Ove replied. "You want to see a good one?"

"Yeah!"

"Okay, watch this one!"

He teed the ball up and booted a sixty-yarder with ease.

"Wow!"

"Let me show you another!"

He teed the ball up and banged one sixty-five yards.

"Want to see another one?"

"No, no . . . you . . . you just stay right here . . . I'm going to get the coach!"

So the player went screaming into the coach's office and yelled, out of breath, "Coach, Coach . . . come out here . . . there's a guy out here kicking sixty—sixty-five-yard field goals!"

The coach almost went into cardiac arrest. He ran to the practice field to meet Ove.

"Let me see you kick," he said.

So Ove chipped a couple of fifty-yarders for him.

"Want to see a long one?" Ove grinned.

"Yeah."

So he backed up and blasted one from way off—in a rush of adrenaline, no one even remembers exactly how far it was.

Coach Wally Bullington signed him on the spot and gave him a half scholarship—which was all he had left to give.

In August I began a nine-week leadership training course for the team and met Ove for the first time. Immediately I sensed that he was special—a very gifted young man who contributed great things to our class of about twenty-five players.

He had an excellent season. In October, for a homecoming game with East Texas State University, he felt the time had come for him to reach his goal.

So the day before the game he and Wilbert Montgomery, later a star on the Philadelphia Eagles, went into Coach Bullington's office and laid out their grand plan.

"Tomorrow, we're going to set *two* world records, Coach!" Ove announced.

"Wilbert is going to set a record for scoring more touchdowns in his collegiate career than anyone else!" (Going into that game, he lacked only one to surpass Lydell Mitchell's record set at Penn State.)

He went on. "And I'm going to kick a field goal farther than anyone has ever done in a game before!"

The coach grinned and told him that if he looked good in their pregame warm-ups, then he'd let him have a shot. Within a few minutes the rest of the players knew about it. Adrenaline began to rush through their veins. No one slept all night.

I conducted pregame sessions and worked on the bench with the players during the game. I'd never seen such excitement. During warm-ups, Ove booted three seventy-yarders. All the kids got pumped even higher, though the opposing team wasn't all that thrilled.

In the second quarter with fourth down on their own forty-one-yard line, the coach turned to Ove. All it took was a slight nod and he shot onto the field for a sixty-nine-yard attempt. The homecoming crowd went crazy—the opposing team looked a bit disoriented.

On the count, the center snapped the ball, the holder smoothly placed it on the tee, and in one swift, fluid motion, Ove's foot smacked the ball. It sounded like someone had scored a direct hit on an elephant's flanks with a high-powered rifle.

The ball went . . . and went . . . almost as if in suspended animation. Then suddenly, the official's arms shot up. A new world's record of sixty-nine yards! The ball would have cleared seventy-five yards easily. Congratulations came in from all over the world. Reporters from dozens of newspapers and wire services called Ove.

Wilbert Montgomery also set a new collegiate record that day. What a day for a Division II college coach.

After the dust settled, Ove and April were our houseguests for the Thanksgiving weekend. Late one evening we were talking, and he casually said to me, "Ron, I didn't kick the football with my foot!" He watched me carefully to see if I was really listening to him. "Oh," I replied.

"No, I kicked it with my head," he said, tapping his temple with his index finger. Then he told me again of his visualization and how he'd learned to program his mind and let it influence the physical action of his body.

When I tell this story, people want to know what happened to Ove. He was injured during his last collegiate game. (He played only his senior year.) Drafted by the Houston Oilers, he wasn't rehabilitated by summer camp. Then Philadelphia brought him in to kick for two games, and he pulled a hamstring. The next summer Dallas brought him into training camp. He had the team made, but Rafael Septien came in with more experience.

Today Ove is very successful in the insurance business.

Why do I tell you Ove's story? Do I think you could go out and kick a record field goal? No, of course not! We all have our talents, gifts, and different possibilities. Ove found his. You have others. I have others. I tell the story to illustrate how your Goal-Seeking Mechanism works. Yes, *yours!*

What Ove has, you have—a brain or mind, a Goal-Seeking Mechanism, that operates like a computer to help us reach goals. We all use this mechanism each day—but most people don't know they do. Every time we drink a cup of coffee or take a bite of food or comb our hair, we use this Mechanism. It's not just for world records.

Ove Johansson had some extraspecial athletic ability, but so have many other kickers who never achieved what he did. It was his ability to visualize what he wanted—to allow his Goal-Seeking Mechanism to work—that made the difference.

It began with his considering that such a feat was possible or *not knowing what was thought to be impossible.* That's the key. He wasn't limited by beliefs that other players had who "knew" what was possible and what wasn't.

So what's the message for you as a leader who wants to get more done through people? How can you help your people with this concept? Let me suggest some action steps.

On a following page, I am printing a Possibility Thinking Formula Worksheet. You may photocopy it and give it to your people. Do the following:

1. Sit down with one or more of your people and explain the formula.

2. Hand each some copies of the worksheet and ask them to pick out a decision, challenge, problem, or situation that they are now experiencing.

3. Ask them to fill in the questions in the worksheet in the next week.

4. Get back to them at a specific time to review their worksheet.

When you get back with them, ask them to do the following.

1. Share their problem, challenge, decision, or situation.
2. Tell how they applied the Possibility Thinking Formula and what happened.
3. Tell what they learned from the experience.

Do this often. Do it until it becomes a thinking habit for them. Look for advances they're making as a result. Reward every small advance, improvement, or success. Continue to reinforce them.

Soon you'll see a different mode of thinking in your people. You'll see people who have been open and searching for new ideas in the past get even better. You'll also see people who are closed, rigid, and boxed in begin to open their minds to creative thinking.

Possibility Thinking Formula Worksheet

1. What problem, challenge, situation, or decision do you either now have, or think you might have soon?_____

_____

_____

2. What would be the best possible outcome to this problem, challenge, decision, or situation?_____

_____

3. Suppose this outcome did happen, how would you feel?

_____

4. What are the chances of this positive outcome actually happening?_____

5. What activities can you do to make sure this positive outcome actually happens?

   a. _____

   _____

   b. _____

   _____

c. _____
   _____
d. _____
   _____

The Challenge Is to Get People to Think

Buckminster Fuller once wrote, "People should think things out fresh and not just accept conventional terms and the conventional way of doing things."

The problem is that not everyone wants to think in new terms. Most people want to think in the same old terms, to stay well within old, comfortable frames of reference.

Moving outside our well-established paradigms can be uncomfortable. It can also cause those who want to control us discomfort. Lots of forces cause people to resist change.

Martin Fisher wrote that, "A conclusion is the place where you get tired of thinking." It echoes Thomas Edison, "There is no expedient to which a man will not go to avoid the real labor of thinking!"

Summing Up

Broadly speaking, your people fall into two categories: Those who think in terms of new possibilities and those who think in terms of limitations.

The possibility thinkers are rare and usually your most productive people. They're highly motivated and always looking for new or better ways to get things done.

If you listen to people, you'll get a pretty good idea of who they are. You'll hear phrases like: "Let's try this new idea;" "Let's find a way to make it work;" "Here's a better way of doing it." Or, conversely, "That's not my department;" "I don't get paid to do that job;" "I just do what they tell me."

I shared a Possibility Thinking Formula and printed a worksheet for you to photocopy and hand out to your people. I suggested that you sit down and review the process with your people and assign them a project of filling in one or more the coming week. Then get back together for another meeting. At this time ask each person to:

1. Share what their problem, situation, challenge, or decision was.
2. How they applied the Possibility Thinking Formula and what happened.
3. What they learned from the experience.

As people share their experiences with the process the past week, you'll see lights come on in their eyes.

Keep this up and you'll see exciting advances in your people's productivity.

How to Gain the Most from This Chapter

Help your people think creatively by having them fill in the Possibility Thinking Worksheets.

You can do this by

1. Explaining the formula to them.
2. Asking them to pick out a decision, challenge, problem, or situation they're now experiencing.
3. Having them fill in the questions in the worksheet during the next week.
4. Having them get back with you to review their worksheet.

People have a powerful Goal-Seeking Mechanism that when they discover and direct helps them dramatically increase their productivity!

10. "The World Makes Way for People Who Know Where They're Going."

Any definite chief aim that is deliberately fixed in the mind and held there, with determination to realize it, finally saturates the entire subconscious mind until it automatically influences the physical action of the body toward the achievement of the goal.

—Napoleon Hill

Goals may be simple or complex. They may be to complete a routine work function or to design a whole new strategic plan for your organization. The goal may be to solve a production problem, raise employee or customer satisfaction levels, or to increase profitability. Regardless of the objective, if you reached it, you followed basically the same process.

So, in a sense, everything you do begins as a goal. The same is true for your people.

Then doesn't it make sense that if your people understand the goal-achievement process, they'll be much more efficient in getting results?

But, what is the system?

A Goal-Achievement System

The following Goal-Achievement System is a step-by-step process which, when followed, will help you define and reach specific goals. As I've said—this process isn't something you *intellectually learn*. Rather it's something you *emotionally experience*. There's a big difference.

The Goal-Achievement System has five parts. They are

1. setting goals,
2. planning strategy,
3. building belief,
4. developing strengths, and
5. evaluating progress.

I've put this into a logical order so that, rather than experiencing goal setting as a hit-or-miss, stab-in-the-dark system, you'll learn a workable process.

Analyze almost any goal you've ever set and reached and you'll discover that you either consciously or unconsciously followed these steps.

Here's a diagram of the system.

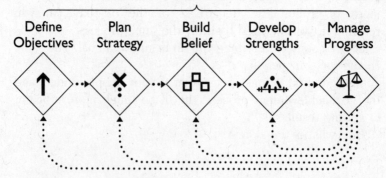

GOAL-ACHIEVEMENT SYSTEM

| Define Objectives | Plan Strategy | Build Belief | Develop Strengths | Manage Progress |

Its simplicity is striking, isn't it? In this system I've brought all the elements of goal achievement together. All you have to do is add desire and action in order to make it work for you.

I challenge you to prove me right or wrong—with your actions.

Getting into Action

Well, until you take action and implement my system, you'll never know whether it'll work for you or not. So . . . let's act!

In order to get into action, I want you to get a pad of paper and a pen or pencil. Please read the following questions and write responses to the ones that are meaningful to you. Okay, no cheating now! Don't just read these and mentally answer or just think about them. Get a pen and paper and write your responses!

Here's the list of questions. Please read each one and write your response to the ones that suggest a desirable response. Some will be meaningful and appropriate; others won't be. Skip over the ones that aren't.

1. How much would you like to weigh?
2. How much money would you like to earn next month or next year?
3. What specific habit would you like to develop?
4. What specific habit would you like to break?
5. What personality trait would you like to develop?
6. What kind of home would you like to own?
7. What improvement would you like to make in your present home?
8. What would you like to do on your next vacation?
9. How would you like to communicate with family members?
10. How would you like to communicate with coworkers?

11. What new office would you like to enjoy?
12. What new position would you like to attain?
13. What new honor would you like to attain?
14. What specific person would you like to have as a closer friend?
15. What improvement in your physical condition would you like to make?
16. What professional or occupational skill would you like to strengthen.
17. What artistic or creative talent would you like to develop?
18. What kind of person would you like to marry?
19. What new hobby would you like to begin?
20. What new activity would you like to begin?
21. What one thing could you do to add more enjoyment to your life?
22. What one goal could you reach that would solve a specific problem you now have?
23. What one goal could you reach that would lessen tension or stress in your life?
24. What one activity could you do that would relieve pressure or worry?
25. What study habits would you like to acquire?
26. What grade-point average would you like to earn?
27. What additional education would you like to have?
28. What physical activity would you like to start?
29. How much money would you like to save each pay period?
30. What specific financial habit would you like to develop?
31. What debts would you like to pay off?
32. How much each month would you like to have when you retire?

33. How much money would you like to leave your family in case of an unexpected death?

34. What charitable contributions would you like to make?

35. How much merchandise, goods, or services would you like to sell? each month, quarter, year?

36. What specific sales skills would you like to strengthen?

37. What would you like to do for your church?

38. What would you like to do for your community?

39. What civic interest or public service would you like to be involved in?

40. How would you like others to describe you?

41. What image would you like to communicate to others?

42. What specific actions can you take to build up your family members?

43. What family activities can you start doing?

44. What common interests can you plan to involve yourself with other family members?

45. What spiritual goals would you like to reach?

46. What spiritual qualities would you like to develop?

47. When people describe you, what three words would you like them to use?

48. What other things would you like to have happen to you in the next year?

Well, these do require some decisions. This is a very important step. Now that you've written answers to the ones that are meaningful to you, here's what I want you to do.

Step 1. Please review your written responses to the questions. Reflect on your answers. Check the six most important ones.

Here's a simple way to arrive at six. Look over all your responses and select the one *most*-important goal. Check it. Then the *next* most-important . . . and so on.

Step 2. When you've selected the six most-important ones, look at each one and put a time limit or date of attainment beside each. Write down the date by which you want to achieve the goal.

Give yourself plenty of time to achieve your goals. Don't be unrealistic. Nothing happens overnight—although many of your goals will come into reality before you expect them to. But for now, be realistic about your target dates.

Step 3. When you've written target dates beside each of your goals, then comes a most important step. Now write your goals into definite statements like this:

"By___(DATE)___I'll___(VERB)_____(GOAL)___!"

Let me give you some examples.

"By May 15, I'll weigh 180 pounds!"

"By July 31, I'll average sales of two hundred thousand dollars' worth of life insurance each month!"

"Beginning January 1, I'll save 10 percent of my income each month!"

"By the end of this next semester I'll have a 3.0 grade-point average!"

You get the message, don't you? Write your goals into a definite statement and put a time limit on each one—write them the way I've suggested. Why? The main reason is that it puts your goal in the form of an active self-suggestion.

Step 4. When you have all six goals written like this, get six 3 × 5 index cards. On each card, write one goal statement on one side. Write them in exciting colors—maybe each in a different color. After writing them on the cards, put a rubber band around them. You're going to carry the cards with you and read them each day.

Goals Should Be Consistent

Conflicting goals can create problems. To prevent this, look at your goals again, and then answer the following questions.

1. Are your goals consistent with your other goals?
2. Are they consistent with your spouse's goals?
3. Are they consistent with your values?
4. Are they consistent with your coworkers' goals?

These are important questions. Many people undermine themselves because their goals conflict with each other or the areas I've just mentioned.

Goals Should Be Statements of the Desired End Result

Many people say they set goals, but upon analysis what they call goals are only vague wishes or hopes.

I've asked many people if they set goals, and they'd reply, "Sure!"

When I ask what goals they set, I get less than specific responses. Like, "My goal is to lose some weight!" Or, "My goal is to get a better job!" Or "My goal is to make more money." Or "My goal is to get a larger home."

Examine all these responses and you'll see a common problem—they aren't specific. They contain words like "more, better, good, some, larger." These words keep their statements from being specific goal statements.

So please watch out for these and other words that keep your goal statements from being specific. Analyze each of the preceding responses and you'll see that none states a specific end result—and that's what a goal is. In the most simple terms I know—*a goal is a statement of the desired end result!*

In the goal-setting seminars that I conduct, I always get around to this simple, basic concept. I start participants from ground zero by having them write down this statement. "A goal is a statement of the desired end result!"

Sounds pretty elementary, doesn't it? It is.

Planning Strategy for Reaching Your Goals

In high school, Kelly Forehand had a goal to be a stockbroker. But during his senior year something happened that appeared to derail his goal. In a high-school football game, he was hit from behind and knocked to the ground. His spinal cord was severed. Lying on the ground, unable to move or breathe, he thought his life was over. An emergency unit got him breathing again, but he became a paraplegic.

Kelly entered extensive therapy and was given an electric wheelchair and even a van that he could drive. He entered college and graduated with a B.B.A. degree in management and a minor in finance. He still had his goal of being a stockbroker. He wanted to work for Merrill Lynch. But there was a problem. They wouldn't give him a job because of his handicap, although the manager's excuse was that he was too young. But that didn't deter him. He kept believing and planning for the day he'd get a job as a broker.

After several months of not finding a job, he came to work in our office doing telephone sales. He was up-front and told me that his ultimate goal was to be with a brokerage firm. I encouraged him to keep the goal while learning as much as he could about sales.

He kept his goal in mind and continued to prepare himself, believing that his chance would come. He read business magazines and the *Wall Street Journal*. He developed work habits and discipline. He kept in contact with a Merrill Lynch broker. He took courses in investments. His chance eventually came— as he knew it would. After four years, a new manager came to the local office. Kelly interviewed with him and got a job. He's been successful, productive, and fulfilled since.

His is a great example of setting a goal and then carefully planning his strategy, believing that at the right time the goal would be reached. He did everything he could to prepare himself for the goal.

The second step of our Goal-Achievement System is planning strategy. Sometimes our strategy can be carefully planned; other times we have to spend time discovering the strategy.

Two Kinds of Goals

There are basically two kinds of goals:

1. Where the strategy or steps of achievement are known, they just have to be taken.
2. Where the strategy or steps are unknown, they have to be discovered.

For some goals, such as building a home, it's pretty simple to plan your strategy. You hire a builder or an architect to design a plan—then execute the steps of the plan. But for goals that don't exist yet—like getting a better job or developing spiritual values—it's often difficult to plan your strategy.

And there are other factors that influence your goal-planning strategy. Here's an important one: Planning is a left-brain logical exercise that requires some concrete organizational ability. But setting goals is usually a right-brain activity—dreaming, believing, and visualizing goal attainment. Often these dimensions don't exist in the same person.

In my experience, people who get emotionally charged about new goals often have problems making clear plans. I've also observed that few people will actually sit down and initiate a goal strategy. Another interesting observation I've made is that those left-brain, detail-minded people who do plot out elaborate goal plans often enjoy *designing* the plan more than *working it out*.

All You Need to Know About Planning

You learned to define goals, how to write them into a definite statement, and put a target date on them.

Let's assume that your target dates are realistic—although it's often hard to know what's realistic and what isn't.

Here are four simple questions that will help you get your planning job done.

1. What's my target date to reach this goal?
2. How can I break my goal down into subgoals or incremental steps?
3. What activities will it take to complete each incremental step?
4. What activities can I perform today?

You'll see that they'll get you a long way down the road in goal planning. They address both the long and short terms. They also bring the reality of goal achievement down to today.

It's easy to fantasize about reaching distant goals and never address the responsibility for achieving them today. But to be successful, the pressure to reach goals should be a daily concern, not something for the future.

Breaking Your Goals Down into Incremental Steps

In 1961 President Kennedy set a goal to put a man on the moon. At the time it sounded impossible, but the president was serious. So he formed a team of scientists to develop the strategy, and the rest is history.

That may have been the most difficult goal that I've seen set and achieved in my lifetime—an incredible event! The team identified each incremental step, developed a strategy, and eight years later, the goal was reached.

How can you break down your goals into subgoals, or incremental steps? Your goal may be to earn a certain sum of money, or to retire, or to have a specific net worth. Or it may be to get a higher degree of education or to lose twenty-five pounds.

These goals can be broken down into incremental steps, or subgoals. Then as each step is realized, you move toward your larger goals.

Often You Can't Plan Out Your Goal Achievement

There are some goals for which you can't plan, because they result from a creative idea. You must have "lightbulb" experiences for these goals to be achieved.

In other words, your unconscious works together with your experience, knowledge, and inner beliefs and . . . zap . . . you wake up in the middle of the night and the way to reach your goal is apparent.

Your answer, or creative idea, didn't pop into your consciousness because you laid out logical plans but because another dimension inside you was also working on the goal. This process gives birth to hunches, flashes of insight, and creative discoveries. All of us use this dimension. Many creative geniuses—Thomas Edison, Albert Einstein, Wernher von Braun—used it extensively.

We use it in simple, everyday ways, too. Each time I've written a book or training course, I've had to select a title. Usually the title isn't selected until after the book is fully written. My goal is always the same—to select an exciting title that either arouses interest or tells what the book is about. Usually I'll spend hours, over a two-or three-month period of time, brainstorming for ideas. I'll write down as many as I can think of, without attempting to come to a decision.

The same thing always happens. I get frustrated because I can't come up with the right one. Then, just when there seems to be no hope, the right title pops into my mind. It pops into my mind at the strangest moments—at 3 A.M., while I'm working out, or while my mind is charged up doing a seminar. In each case, my Goal-Seeking Mechanism steers me to the achievement of the goal.

Building Belief in Your Goals

Several years ago, our firm conducted about twenty-five three-day Psycho-Cybernetics seminars for the Illinois Division of Vocational Rehabilitation. We trained unemployed disabled people to get jobs and keep them.

We saw miracles happen to many of the people. Let me tell you a couple of stories. See if you can pinpoint *why* they changed.

The first seminar was at the University of Chicago, where seventy-five handicapped people had been enrolled by their caseworkers or counselors. Most of the people were from south Chicago, and the first morning it looked like a death march. No enthusiasm, no excitement, no life. We had paraplegics, quadriplegics, blind people, deaf people, amputees—all kinds of disabilities.

As the participants were filing in, I began to feel depressed. I lost my usual preseminar "up." I began the session by reaching down into my reserve and pulling up as much emotional energy as I could. As I looked into a sea of dead faces, I connected with one—bright, smiling, and giving me massive nods of approval. So I focused on him.

At the first break, I found out his name was Henry Mortensen. Henry was in a wheelchair, looked around thirty, and had one of the brightest smiles I'd ever seen. I found out that day that he'd never had a job and had been on welfare for several years. I'd never seen anyone more positive or anyone who threw himself into a seminar more than Henry.

The first day we gave them some assessment instruments and tried to get them to identify their strengths. The second day everyone set goals, and the third day they developed plans to reach their goals. Laced throughout the three days were team-building exercises, along with lots of discussion and interaction at their tables.

In the three days, the whole group just came alive. Skeptical at first, they soon believed I was sincerely interested in them.

They dropped their defenses and really got into the flow of things.

Several of them kept in touch for a few years afterward. I got letters telling of weight loss, new jobs, and things for their homes.

About a year after the seminar I got a letter from Henry Mortensen. He began his letter by saying, "You probably don't remember me, but . . ."

He was wrong. How could I have forgotten him? He went on to say that he'd set three goals during the seminar. They were

1. to get a business of his own,

2. to earn over nine thousand dollars the first year, and

3. to get married.

He continued: "If you'll look at this letterhead, you'll see that I've accomplished my first goal."

The letterhead read, "Sales on Wheels . . . Henry Mortensen, President."

Henry explained that he'd gotten a motorized wheelchair and was selling home-care products door-to-door. He then proudly told me that he had exceeded his second goal—which was to earn nine thousand dollars the first year. "As for my third goal . . ." he finished, explaining how he'd enrolled in a dance club for handicapped people, met a young woman, and they were soon to be married.

What a story! I read and reread the letter many times. I kept asking myself the same question: Considering the fact that the handicap that had caused him to be unemployed and on welfare hadn't changed at all . . . but his whole life had changed . . . the question I kept asking myself was, "What was it about Henry that changed?"

What was it? You're right! The only thing that changed about him was his *beliefs!* His attitude! His mental paradigm. Nothing else had changed—except, of course, his whole life!

Developing Strengths to Reach Your Goals

Often, before a goal can be reached, we must develop some personal strengths. And the same is true for corporate or organizational goals. Developing strengths is part of the price of goals.

During goal-achievement seminars over the years, I've asked participants to assess the strengths their goals will require.

Here are four kinds of strengths you may have to develop in order to reach your goals:

1. Attitudes
2. Habits
3. Skills

Attitudes

Our attitudes are how we think—about ourselves and others. It's a mind-set, a belief system, a viewpoint. We commonly characterize attitudes as positive or negative. Of course, they can be either, but those are only two dimensions of the way we think.

Our attitudes, or our views toward people, situations, and circumstances, are the product of many things: our education, experiences, culture, training, mentoring or modeling of others, heritage. How do we view things? How do we explain who we are and how we fit into the world around us? These describe our attitude.

Habits

A habit is an automatic response, something you do unconsciously, instinctively, without thinking.

We're all creatures of habits. From the way we brush our

teeth, comb our hair, and put on our shoes in the morning, to the way we do our jobs. Good habits cause good results; bad ones cause bad results. It's cause and effect.

Success is usually the result of certain habits. Once a habit is formed, our automatic mechanism takes over and unconsciously causes us to perform in a habitual way in different situations.

Most successful people have developed good time-management habits. Procrastination, indecisiveness, and inaction are weak habits that can be changed.

Years ago, when reading *Success Through a Positive Mental Attitude*, I was forced to confront my habit of procrastination. Stone and Hill recommended memorizing the self-suggestion, "Do it now!" and saying the words over and over until they became permanently imprinted on our minds. Whenever we see something that needs to be done, we can flash this mental command, "Do it now!" to ourselves.

I added another suggestion: "When I see something that needs to be done, I do it!" Then I repeated this to myself fifty times each morning and fifty times each afternoon. After this repetitive programming, every time I saw something that needed to be done, this command would flash into my conscious mind: "When I see something that needs to be done, I do it!" I would then follow through with action. That's how I developed a habit.

All of our habits form the same way! Habits are formed by consciously doing certain actions repetitively, over time. It takes *practice* and *time lapse* for habits to form. It usually takes a minimum of twenty-one days of practicing an action before a habit emerges.

Habits are broken by substituting one action for another— repeatedly over time.

Habits are formed or broken by consciously acting repetitively over time. That's important to know.

What habits will it take to reach your goals? What habits will you have to break? What will you replace them with? As you review your goals, ask yourself these questions and record your responses. This process can open the doors to your new goals—and not doing it might keep the doors of your new goals permanently closed!

Skills

Skills are developed abilities. Reading, writing, and arithmetic are skills. Playing golf, painting a picture, sewing a button on a shirt, performing a root canal, doing laser surgery to remove a cataract, doing a heart bypass, riding a bicycle are all skills.

In order to reach your goals, you'll have to develop skills. Regardless of whether your goal is to be a legal secretary, accountant, computer programmer, or auto technician, you'll need skills.

A good question, then, is "What skills must I develop in order to reach my goals?" The skills that you define will then become subgoals. As you ask this question of yourself (and, more importantly, as you get answers), you'll discover some important factors in reaching your goals.

Managing Progress to Reach Your Goals

In order to manage your progress, here are four action guides:

1. Review goals
2. Proceed
3. Revise
4. Recycle

Let's consider each step. You'll see how easy they are and how they fit into our system.

Review Goals

The first action guide for managing your goal progress is to *review your goals*. You can do this by reading your goals daily or weekly.

Each time you read your goals ask yourself some questions. Ask:

1. Where am I with this goal—what is my progress?
2. Are all my goals still important to me?
3. How can I best use my time?
4. What subgoals should I have already reached to take me to my main goals?

Until this process is internalized into your habits, I'd recommend that you go through it daily, then two or three times each week.

As you review your goals, you'll discover only three appropriate responses. For each of your goals, you'll want to

1. Proceed
2. Revise
3. Recycle

Proceed

You'll *proceed* with your goal if you still want to achieve it, believe that it's possible, and are willing to keep developing the strengths to reach it.

In other words, your goal is still important to you. You still want to reach it but haven't had enough time. So you proceed. You keep building belief and developing the strengths you need—realizing that when everything comes together you'll either see your goal within reach or have reached it!

Revise

The second appropriate response after you review your goals is to *revise* them. I'm always amazed how fast some goals become realized. I often look back at goal booklets in which I've set goals. Most of them have happened—and often sooner than I expected.

Another discovery that strikes me is that many of my goals had to be revised. They had to be revised either *up* or *down*. Often I discover, after setting and working on goals for a while, that they aren't consistent with my values, my priorities, or some of my other goals. For these reasons, I need to revise them, to change them. Rewrite them and keep working on the system—planning strategy, building belief, developing strengths, and managing your progress.

Recycle

The third appropriate response you can take after you review your goals is to *recycle*. When you recycle, you redefine your goals and go back through your Goal-Achievement System. You do the following:

1. Begin with new goals

2. Plan strategy

3. Build belief

4. Develop strengths

5. Manage progress

You may also recycle when you've had a lapse of interest or have once set a goal and later stalled out.

It's common to set a goal, be serious about it for a while, and then lose interest. Or maybe new events cause it to slip from your priorities. Then later you get excited about it again.

The Goal-Achievement System Is a System

The Goal-Achievement System that I've presented is powerful and workable. When you follow the system and manage your progress, you'll be amazed at how quickly some of your goals materialize.

You'll find that this system is just that—a system! It has built-in checks, balances, and policing agents. It has its own internal guidance systems. It's fully functioning; all you have to do is punch the start-up button, activate, and maintain the system; and it'll work for you.

I've conducted enough seminars in goal setting to know about getting people to follow this system. One common response is, "Yeah, well, this may all be true, but there's more to life than just reaching material goals!"

I agree. There's more to life than cars, houses, clothes, and money. I'll be the first to admit it. Spiritual dimensions and family and personal relationships are infinitely more important. But these inner qualities are also goals, and you can use this system to attain them.

Practice This System Until You Do the Steps Automatically

I'll admit this five-step system looks mechanical, with many rules and guides. I've designed it that way for a purpose. The reason is so nothing is left to chance, that we cover all of the bases.

What I know from experience is that if you follow this system to the letter—defining specific goals and then working through the steps—you'll experience success. When you do, you'll *emotionally* believe in the process. You'll only believe that it'll really work for you when you see it working for you. Then, with time and experience, the whole Goal-Achievement System will be-

come automatic. You'll perform many of the steps unconsciously.

Achieving this mind-set will take time and practice, but with
repetition you'll instinctively begin to think and act in a goal-
focused way. I've shared this Goal-Achievement System with
many thousands of people. I've used it myself. I know it works.
I know it'll work for you and for your people!

Summing Up

In this chapter, I have presented a Goal-Achievement System.
It's a process that you and your people can use to facilitate the
reaching of any goal, objective, decision, or problem resolution.

The Goal-Achievement System becomes a road map to follow for greater productivity. As your people understand the
stages they must go through in order to reach goals, they'll
naturally become more efficient and productive.

Earlier in this book, I presented the concept of your Goal-
Seeking Mechanism—the onboard computer in your head that
unconsciously steers you to the goals or targets you set for it.
Understand the power and function of this mechanism and
you'll see how the Goal-Achievement System is the blueprint
that will activate it. The system gives you a process on which
to focus your powerful Goal-Seeking Mechanism.

The Goal-Achievement System helps harness all your mental
and creative energies so you can then focus on your targets or
objectives.

How to Gain the Most from This Chapter

In order to benefit from the power of this chapter, here are
some action steps to follow.

1. Read and digest the chapter—especially the Goal-
   Achievement System—focusing on the chapter content for
   a week.

2. Follow the instructions and go through the system yourself—writing down your goals and following my suggestions.

3. Share the system with your associates. Help them identify their own goals.

4. Get feedback from them at the end of the week. Find out the kinds of goals they set and how they're working through the system.

5. Encourage them to apply the system to any work process, objective problem, or decision.

People will produce 40 percent more efficiently when they are part of a positive, harmonious team who share a common purpose.

11. The Whole Is Greater Than the Sum of Its Parts.

The very essence of all power to influence lies in getting the other person to participate. The mind that can do that has a powerful leverage on his human world.

—HARRY A. OVERSTREET

Teamwork is essential for getting more done through people. People maximize their potential when they work together in a spirit of unity and harmony toward a common goal or purpose. When they do, a power develops that's greater than the sum of the individuals' powers.

It's called *synergy!*

The Ritz-Carlton Hotel in Phoenix discovered this powerful principle recently. Typically, hotel rooms are cleaned by one person, then a floor supervisor checks on how well each room has been cleaned. In their quest for quality improvement, they asked the maids how they thought they could improve their work. And, as is often the case, the people cleaning knew much more about process improvement than their managers who only observe.

They rose to the challenge. They suggested two changes.

1. That they be allowed to work in teams of two rather than one person cleaning in a room.
2. That they eliminate the floor supervisors and take team responsibility for the job's being done right.

So, they were allowed to try the strategies. First, they asked to select their own team members. Some were mother/daughter teams, others were sisters or friends.

Immediately, quality improved. After the routine was set, they were able to get all the rooms cleaned 40 percent faster by working in teams. Since they asked for and assumed responsibility for their thoroughness, supervisors' jobs were eliminated, which added to the cost savings and efficiency.

In this case, the power of synergy increased their productivity 40 percent. Pretty exciting, isn't it?

But that was only a part of the increase. The people involved developed better attitudes and self-esteem. Their pride in their work increased, as did their job satisfaction.

Synergy—the Whole Is Greater Than the Sum of Its Parts

Synergy is such a fascinating concept, which few of us know enough about.

I read a story once that illustrates its power. Most of us have seen the cleaning detergent, 20 Mule Team Borax. Remember the picture on the box? It's a drawing of twenty mules pulling two huge wagons and a smaller one out of a borax pit in Death Valley, California, in the 1800s. I saw this for years before I knew the significance of the picture. I was fascinated when I learned the true story.

For years the hearty wagoneers used twelve mules to pull the wagonload of borax from an open pit and several miles to a railroad. For a long time no one questioned it. Twelve mules were needed and that was that. Then a creative thinker, who wasn't content to live with the conventional wisdom, began experimenting. He found that he could add eight mules to the twelve-mule team and with twenty mules could pull *two* huge wagons, plus a water wagon. By adding eight mules to the twelve, it more than doubled the pulling capacity. It created a new power.

That's synergy—where two or more people or forces work together in a cooperative spirit, the total power becomes greater than the sum of the individual powers.

If you've ever been part of an athletic team where everyone pulled together in pursuit of a win, you know how exhilarating it can be. Momentum is a common word used to describe the result of synergism.

Teamwork Begins with Having a Common Goal or Purpose

Before team spirit, momentum, or synergy can happen, people must share a common goal, vision, or purpose.

Today, many organizations are committing to customer service. Some espouse it because it looks impressive on a mission statement on the reception-room wall, and no one really heeds it. The leaders of other companies see the value of a customer focus but don't know how to align their people with this vision and move them into its daily practice.

Other managers clearly articulate their direction to their people, walk their talk, and model customer-focused behaviors. For them, a customer focus is a value, not a strategy. It's not just something they preach; it's something they practice.

When managers have this *value* of focusing on customer needs, they select people who have the same values, then train them to ask:

1. Who are their customers?
2. What are their needs?

3. How can your organization fill those customer needs?

4. How can their job roles work with others to create customer satisfaction and ultimately customer loyalty?

When your people understand these four things, they are in a position to focus their skills and energies on efficiently doing their jobs.

The Paradox of Having a Customer Focus

There's a paradox here. When people focus on serving others, or working toward something that creates value for others, they like themselves better. Their self-esteem, energy, enthusiasm, and job commitment all increase. They become more productive and fulfilled.

That's the paradox. When we focus on something outside ourselves, we feel better about ourselves.

Sidney Powell said it well, "Try to forget yourself in the service of others. For when we think too much of ourselves and our own interests, we easily become despondent. But when we work for others, our efforts return to bless us."

Leaders have the ability to inspire motivation in their people. To the extent the common purpose creates value for others, the people are energized. Their interest, enthusiasm, and energy quickens.

The foundation for synergistic teamwork is laid when the following factors are in place:

1. A clear purpose that creates value for customers or other stakeholders outside the organization.

2. A well-defined strategy for attaining objectives.

3. Communication of this purpose and strategy and the value it creates.

4. How each person's job role fits into this purpose.

5. Reporting and accountability expectations.

Corporate Values

I am convinced that corporate and personal values powerfully influence productivity and profitability.

Strong corporate values are demonstrated when leaders believe and practice the following priorities; when they are both talked and walked:

1. To satisfy their customers and thus create apostles.
2. To provide a meaningful work environment and opportunity for their people,
3. To make a profit.

When you and your management team prioritize in these three ways, your customers will definitely know it. Your people will see it and be impressed. Your profits will be maximized. (Obviously, if products, marketing, and other functions are efficiently managed.)

Healthy and sustained profits come to individuals or organizations as value is created for customers. Value causes customer satisfaction, and it's necessary for customer loyalty.

Southwest Airlines is an excellent corporate example of walking their talk. From a single plane carrying passengers from Dallas to Houston, Texas, to the present, they have enjoyed spectacular growth—both in cities served and in number of passengers served. They are first in customer satisfaction, on-time departures, and baggage arrival. My guess is that they are also number one in the airline industry in employee satisfaction. Certainty, they are the only airline that has enjoyed profitability every year for the last twenty-plus years. Employee satisfaction and loyalty and customer satisfaction and loyalty all drive profitability.

Southwest Airlines has some pretty simple values to which they conscientiously adhere. Herb Kelleher, the founding guru and head cheerleader, makes no bones about these values like, "Employee satisfaction is number one in importance."

"Customers aren't always right," he remarks. "Sometimes they're wrong and we don't want them as customers if they abuse our other passengers or employees."

Southwest spends lots of energy selecting people. They hire sharp, energetic, young people who are friendly and can mix work with fun. Flight attendants and counter agents, the jobs with the most customer contacts, are allowed to be creative and innovative. They do unboring things like sing songs or recite poetry to the passengers. When explaining the routine departure procedures to passengers, they create lines that make it fun like, "Please fasten the seat belt tightly across your lips, er hips . . ." Or, "If you're seated next to a child . . . or someone acting like a child . . . fasten your seat belt first, then theirs." They're trained to say, in a sense, "Hey this could be routine, redundant, boring stuff, so let's just enjoy ourselves and have some fun."

Despite the company's rapid growth and thousands of employees, they have kept a family atmosphere. Herb Kelleher can still recall a huge number of their employees' names. He's incredible! I attended a meeting not long ago where he spoke. There must have been fifteen hundred people in attendance, many of them Southwest employees. He seemed to know all their names as he hugged them and let them know that he valued them. He unabashedly told them how much he loved them.

Building and running a business is never simple. There are difficulties at every level of growth, but Southwest Airlines is a living example that basic values and profitability are inseparably linked, and that they can be sustained from the inception of an organization into its mature growth stages.

All you have to do is look at the airlines that went broke to see what a remarkable job Kelleher has done.

The basic values he has instilled in his people are:

1. Hire people who like people.

2. Make employee satisfaction number one, which will ensure high customer satisfaction.

3. Create a unique travel experience for customers at a low price.

4. Make passengers feel important and noticed.

5. Set and reach high standards of on-time performance.

In the last thirty-five years I have flown many other airlines, most of which aren't in existence now. Very few communicated any uniqueness or caused me to feel that I'd experienced special treatment.

How Teams Are Developed

Let's use a sports metaphor to analyze the elements of a team. To develop this model, let's go back to your high-school or college team. What made it successful? I'll bet I can guess some elements.

1. *A name and a uniform*—an identity, a uniquely crafted distinction that differentiated them from other teams.

2. *A purpose*—to win games and bring honor and recognition to their school.

3. *A coach*—to set the vision, to train, and communicate a belief that goals will be reached.

4. *Captains*—leaders who understand the goals of both coaches and players and lead players by example.

5. *Players*—a group of people with diverse skills and abilities who are yielding their own glory to the success of the team.

6. *Basic training and conditioning*—to equip players to know what and how to perform their functions.

7. *A game plan*—clear action statements that if executed properly should lead to victory.

8. *Coaching and practice*—inspecting performance and continual development of each individual's skills.

9. *Scores and statistics*—specific measurements that tell the team how they're doing.

10. *Rewards*—sharing the thrill of victory and the responsibility of continual learning and improvement.

Not a bad model for corporate teams, is it?

Take a moment and review the preceding ten elements that make up a team. While your mind is back at your old-school metaphor mode, reflect how these ten factors were played out by your old team. As you reflect about it, how well were they played out?

Then look at your old rivals. Think about the ones who were consistently good and the ones who were consistently also-rans. How did they stack up in these ten elements?

How *does* your organization currently rate in these ten factors? Which ones are your strongest? Which need improvement? What might happen if you took this list I've just given you, reproduced it, and asked your people to come up with ideas about how your organization can adopt some of them?

That "Something Else"

Remember in earlier chapters, I suggested that leadership is the sum of certain traits . . . and *something else*? Have you determined what that "something else" is yet?

As you look at the preceding ten factors, you can put all ten of these elements together and you will certainly have a team, but you won't necessarily have *synergy* or *momentum* unless you have that "something else."

I have led you through many thoughts and discoveries so far in this book. Enough, if you're prepared to uncover it, to find out for yourself that chemical ingredient that serves as a catalyst, transforming other ingredients into a more powerful state.

What are you discovering? Keep searching.

Momentum and Team Synergy

Remember in your physics class that you learned, "A body in motion tends to stay in motion, and a body at rest tends to stay at rest?" Who was that—Darwin, Newton, Rip Van Winkle, or your local mortician? Well, whichever, it's an interesting concept.

You've also noticed that a winning team keeps on winning, and a losing team keeps on losing. You've also heard many times the term "a winning tradition."

What is a "winning tradition?" What is *momentum?* Where does it come from? Why can't it be measured or predicted? How do we better understand *synergism?*

To answer these questions, let's go back to a model I presented to you in chapter five.

Remember the three dimensions of human behavior? See the following diagram.

Intellectual
"I Think"

Emotional
"I Feel"

Creative/Unconscious
"I Am"

In chapter five I presented this model mainly as a personal one. Let's expand it a bit and translate it into a team example.

Teams that excel and play at high levels, or in "The Zone," communicate through different channels than other teams. Invariably they move past conscious intellectual thought to operate at a subconscious, "free flow" level.

Let me illustrate different levels of communication like this.

Conscious/Intellectual Communication

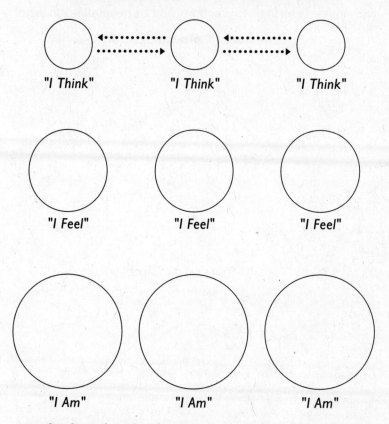

In this logical, rational state, people know how to do their jobs and focus on them and don't necessarily see how they fit into the bigger picture. They're often process- or project-focused. Communication is with words and directives.

Theoretically, if everyone knows how to do their jobs, and does them, success will result. But, why doesn't it always happen? How about people who know what to do but have negative attitudes, so their productivity suffers despite their knowledge.

Why do some people become angry and upset with each other, causing logical advice to go unheeded. If you're coming from a different dimension, miscommunication takes place, and you're not even on the same page. Notice how people can fail to communicate by listening, thinking, and speaking to different dimensions—from logic to emotions, and from emotions to logic.

Emotional Communication

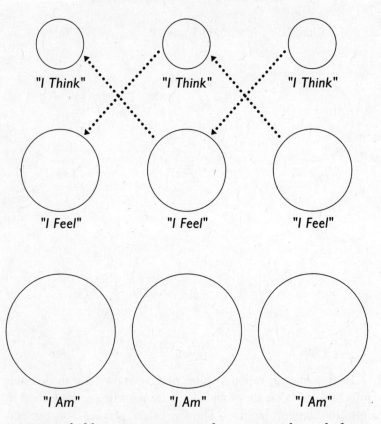

You probably communicate with your people with *logic*, which they don't hear because they're in an *emotional* mode. Emotions like preoccupation with job security or lack of it, conflicts with other people, etc.

You say things like, "Look, if you'll only follow these guidelines, you'll be more productive." But your people are silently saying, "Easy for you to say . . . my wife is leaving me and taking the kids and you talk to me about logic? I'm dying on the inside!"

Or you may say to your salesperson, "If you'll just make 30 percent more calls, you'll increase your sales 30 percent!" But your salesperson is consumed with call reluctance and is emotionally frozen. Your logic totally misses the mark. You're communicating from a logical base, and they're operating from an emotional one.

Or, people can communicate from emotional level to emotional level. It may be positive or negative—enthusiasm, acceptance, and positive reinforcement; or anger, argumentativeness, and hostility. You may be experiencing stresses or pressures to produce more, and you call your people in and give them a shape-up-or-ship-out speech. You rattle a few cages and shake up the troops, triggering emotions and causing fear, resentment, or panic. Before you know it, both you and your people are operating from a negative, emotional motivation which ruins team synergism. So negatively or positively it would look like this.

Emotional Communication

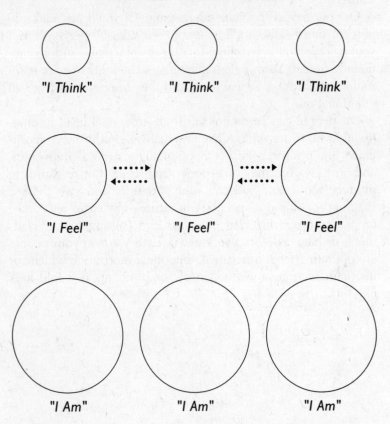

Then, to go deeper, when momentum or synergy exists in an organization or team, a much deeper level of communication exists—from the Creative/Unconscious to the Creative/Unconscious. From the "I Am" to the "I Am." This level of communication is characterized by mutual trust, respect, and concern. It's when people are singing from the same song sheet.

This point is illustrated by the following model.

Unconscious Communication

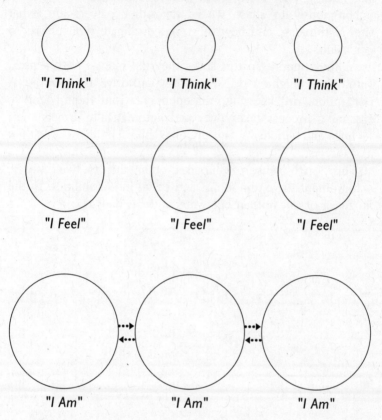

This level of communication or human response exists when people are in "The Zone," when that illusive, powerful force is present that transcends the sum of people's natural abilities. It's when people are in "flow." This state of synergy is characterized by people committed to common goals who demonstrate unity, harmony, and mutual respect and belief in others. When people subordinate their own egos and recognition to the success of the team.

In this state people seem to perform effortlessly with unusual energy. They easily reach their "second wind." They seem unconsciously to sense where the other players are, what they're thinking, and how they can coordinate their efforts to get results.

As they operate in this state, they tap into a "sixth sense." Intuition is heightened. New energy and drive are released. A perception, or "knowing," independent from their cognitive reasoning process takes over and automatically directs their feelings and actions. A sagacity or perspicacity takes over then and directs.

This "sixth sense" influences other factors like energy, achievement drive, emotions, and belief in possibilities. In the language of our human behavior model it does this.

"Sixth Sense" Communication

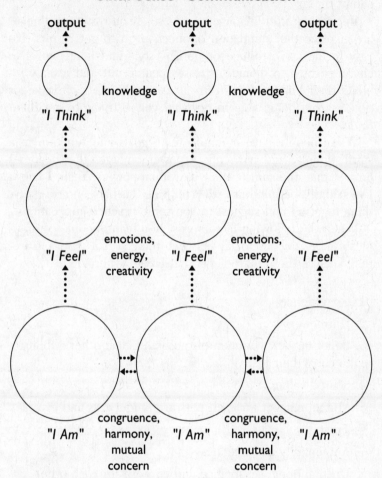

Impacting the Bottom Line

Let's begin by understanding that the purpose of any team is to win or produce consistently. Most all of us are, in one way or another, charged with getting measurable results. Results count!

But all too often managers focus solely on results and never lay in place the foundation or mechanism to get results. It's easy to have a "produce or perish" style and ignite negative charges which, of course, stresses people out and usually inhibits their ability to perform at a high level. It often keeps people from being able to do what you're trying to get them to do.

When people have common team goals and function in a spirit of unity and harmony, a power emerges that becomes greater than the sum of their individual powers. Yeah, I know, I've said this before, but I want to bring this back and tie everything together and suggest to you some practice applications.

When the following factors exist in a team, people communicate more unconsciously between their "I Am" levels. Carefully analyze these ingredients that create synergy.

1. Congruence

2. Harmony

3. Belief in their common purpose and each other's ability to carry their loads

4. Shared values

5. Mutual respect for each person's uniqueness and diversity

6. Trust

7. Authenticity and openness

8. Unconditional acceptance and concern for each other

9. Willingness to subordinate individual egos to the good of the team

10. Expectation of winning

When these ten factors pervade a team's environment and with time and incubation, a psychic power emerges that pulls everyone together. As this transformation occurs, it sparks enthusiasm, energy, zeal, hustle, and esprit de corps in the people.

This new life-form, when combined with knowledge, yields productivity and results.

Cause and Effect

Everything is cause and effect! Achieving success, in whatever you do, is the result of what precedes it. This whole book is designed to let you lay the groundwork that will produce quality, productivity, success, or profitability—whichever is appropriate for you.

Take a few minutes and rate your organizational environment in light of the ten ingredients that I've just mentioned. Search back in this book and select specific strategies or actions that you can do to strengthen the ones you feel need to be done.

Also, take a look at the Organizational Productivity Survey on the next page. Score yourself on each area. Then score your organization as you think your senior managers would; and third, score your organization as you think your employees or associates would. After you have scored each one, connect the appropriate dots from top to bottom, forming three separate curves. Compare the three.

Organizational Productivity Survey

1. All our people understand and feel good about the overall vision, mission, and purpose of our organization.
   1　　2　　3　　4　　5　　6　　7　　8　　9　　10

2. All our people feel good about the values and integrity of our managers and peer associates.
   1　　2　　3　　4　　5　　6　　7　　8　　9　　10

3. All our people feel good about their job stability and security.
   1　　2　　3　　4　　5　　6　　7　　8　　9　　10

4. All our people communicate freely and openly with each other.
   1　　2　　3　　4　　5　　6　　7　　8　　9　　10

5. All our people feel comfortable taking risks, being innovative and creative.
   1　　2　　3　　4　　5　　6　　7　　8　　9　　10

6. All our people know who our customers are, how we generate revenue, and what our unique advantages are over our competition.
   1　　2　　3　　4　　5　　6　　7　　8　　9　　10

7. All our people clearly understand their individual work processes and how they fit into our organizational success.
   1　　2　　3　　4　　5　　6　　7　　8　　9　　10

8. All our people are constantly striving to improve their work processes.
   1　　2　　3　　4　　5　　6　　7　　8　　9　　10

9. All our salespeople understand and practice customer-needs-focused selling.
   1　　2　　3　　4　　5　　6　　7　　8　　9　　10

10. Our organization is a totally customer-focused one.
    1　　2　　3　　4　　5　　6　　7　　8　　9　　10

Set Up Success Support Systems

A success support system can be formed by dividing your people into groups of four to six compatible groups. Here are some suggestions that will work wonders for them.

1. Meet once a week for one hour.
2. Before each meeting, each group must read a chapter in a self-help book, listen to an audiocassette message, or practice some quality-improvement action.
3. Get together, elect a discussion leader, and do the following:
   a. Each person shares what he/she learned from the book, tape, or action and how they practiced it, or plan to.
   b. Listen carefully and encourage each person.
   c. Spend the balance of the time pointing out strengths and growth they see in each person.

When this is conducted in a totally positive environment, where no arguments or criticism is allowed, magic occurs quickly.

These support groups can be held during the lunch hour or at other times that fit your schedule. When people get together on a regularly scheduled basis, in a positive, noncritical environment, growth occurs within three to four weeks.

These support groups can powerfully influence your people's productivity, communication, and individual self-esteem.

Summing Up

In this chapter I have reminded you of the concept of *synergism*. It's a force that develops when people work together with unity and harmony toward a common goal.

We thought about some examples of how synergy, momentum, or "flow" increases people's productivity beyond mathematically correct logic. We thought about your old school team and the ingredients that made it successful and kept it being that way. I gave you some factors for developing teams.

Having a customer focus helps organizations develop synergism. Getting people to focus on their value to others causes a transformation to occur.

I challenged you to think of that "something else" that I mentioned at the beginning of this book. If we were sitting together talking now, what would you tell me this "something else" is?

I've funneled many years of learning and observation into this chapter. I hope it challenges you to dig deeply and develop a clearer understanding of what creates synergy and momentum and, bottom line, what helps you help your people get more done.

How to Gain the Most from This Chapter

To dig deeper into this chapter's power, I suggest you spend a week doing the following:

1. Read and reread the chapter several times.
2. Evaluate your organization in the ten factors that when they exist help your people communicate on their deep "I Am" level.
3. Look at the Organizational Productivity Survey. Rate it how: (1) you'd rate it, (2) your senior managers would rate it, and (3) how your employees or associates would rate it.
4. Understand my outline for setting up Success Support Systems and test its effectiveness with your people.

This will be a very exciting and productive week for you as you take action on these ideas.

People and events stand in the wings of life awaiting direction from the power of your beliefs and expectations.

12. "Belief and Philosophy Constitute a Transcendent Factor"

Man is what he believes.

—ANTON CHEKHOV

Years ago the McKinsey Foundation Lecture Series, sponsored by Graduate School of Business, Columbia University, held a lecture by Thomas J. Watson Jr. of IBM fame. The lecture was titled "A Business and Its Beliefs—The Ideas That Helped Build IBM."

In this lecture Mr. Watson made this observation about the success of the great organization he built.

> Belief and philosophy constitute a transcendent factor which outweighs technology, economic resources, or anything else, in achieving success.
>
> This then is my thesis, I firmly believe that any organization, in order to survive and achieve success, must have a sound set of beliefs on which it premises all its policies and actions . . .
>
> In other words, the basic philosophy, spirit, and drive of an organization have far more to do with its

relative achievements than do technological or economic resources, organizational structure, innovation, and timing. All these things weigh heavily in success. But they are, I think, *transcended* by how strongly the people in the organization believe in its basic precepts and how faithfully they carry them out.

Might I suggest that you take a moment and read Mr. Watson's statement again?

Powerful words! By a brilliant man with obvious business savvy. This is a very strong statement that there is a *transcending* factor that outweighs all other assets considering he was in the technology business.

Transcend! Interesting word. Here's what Webster says it means: "to go beyond the limits of possible experience, to exceed, to be superior, to surprise, to excel, to go beyond human knowledge."

Whoa! Stop the action! What's going on here? The leader of an organization dedicating its whole future to technology and organizational excellence saying that there's something *more* important than those! Not only *more* important, but *far surpassing*, and something that can take an organization beyond the current limits of human thinking and knowledge!

I know, that was in 1965, and maybe you think all that has changed since then. But, foundational things have not changed.

Could Mr. Watson's point be as true today as it was then? Could he have stated a foundational truth that never changes? That what he said always has influenced the success of organizations and always will?

In the two-thousand-plus organizations my people have worked with, I see this clearly. Organizations and individuals that are vital, healthy, and growing are the ones that have a "sound set of beliefs on which they premise all their policies and actions . . ."

Organizations and individuals who are truly "customer-focused" have a zest or positive spirit that others don't. People who see meaning in their jobs have more energy. People with an external rather than internal focus, without question, are happier and more fulfilled. Employee morale and esprit de corps can often be dramatically increased when they focus on the end-result benefits they cause people to enjoy rather than on their process or product.

When management values people over processes, a transcendence occurs. When processes are valued over people (which has clearly happened), the creative dimensions within people are shut off.

This was why the quality movement of the late eighties and early nineties didn't live up to its expectations. It often caused people to focus on the process and not the people involved, nor the end-result benefit to customers. They became too myopic, too nearsighted, too self-focused.

An Organization's Core Beliefs and Values Are a Transcendent Factor

Earlier I wrote about your core beliefs and values. At that point it may have sounded like I was preaching a sermon. Since then I have given you a number of processes for understanding and building people. I shared the ingredients of leadership. I mentioned, though, that leadership is more than the sum of the individual parts. I alluded to that "something else" that when added to the ingredients helps make up the whole.

This chapter will close the loop and bring everything together.

I believe that as a practical, hard-nosed, dollars-and-cents business practice, positive beliefs and values modeled by leaders and lived out by the people in organizations is a *transcendent* factor.

Transcendent as it goes beyond reason, logic, and analytical cognition.

Life Paradoxes

Life has many paradoxes—eternal truths that endure regardless of how they conflict with conventional wisdom.

I have long been intrigued by this paradox from the Master Teacher, Jesus, "It is more blessed (happy) to give than to receive!" Another paradox He mentioned was, "Give and it will be given to you: good measure, pressed down, shaken together, running over, will be put into your lap. For the measure you give will be the measure you get back."

I believe that these statements that fly in the face of conventional wisdom, are eternal truths—paradoxes, serendipities. I've observed the lives of many people. Some very happy and fulfilled; others miserable. The traditional trappings of success (money, large homes, fancy cars, etc.) seemed to have no relationship with happiness, joy, zest for life, and fulfillment. I've found wealthy people who were happy and contented. I've found others who were depressed to the point of desperation. I've known happy people who had little in the way of possessions and unhappy people who commiserated about their lack of funds, thinking that if they could just win the lottery they would be happy and life would be wonderful.

I met a man once who told me he was worth $50 million, and in the next breath said he had no friends; that he had two small children by a second marriage, and that they were the only two people in the world who loved him—his wife didn't, his parents didn't. I've never seen a more miserable person.

The same week, one of my friends lost everything in the Texas oil crash. His net worth plummeted from around $25 million to $6 million in debt. Over the next several years, it became clear that he and his wife were just as happy with nothing as they had been with a lot of money. They lost their ten-thousand-plus-square-foot home and moved into a one-bedroom apartment. They said the process was a cleansing one that helped them focus on what's important.

I've observed corporate paradoxes where organizations conscientiously focused on creating products and services that cause the most *customer* value. In most cases, they became profitable, highly productive organizations. They enjoyed a foundational health and vitality that then *transcended* the logic of what they did.

Sensing this, my business partner, Bernard Petty, and I decided to give back a specific portion of our corporate profits. We shared the concept with some of our associates and asked a group to flesh out a name and guidelines. They named it Project Champions.

Project Champions is a wonderful activity. Any of our hundreds of certified facilitators can donate their time to conducting our ten-week Managing Goal Achievement Course for underprivileged people, and we will donate all the necessary materials. We hold courses all around the country for diverse audiences—abused women, teens at risk, teenage mothers, Boys Ranch, etc.

We see incredible growth in many of the people taking control of their lives, dealing with abusers, setting goals for the future, and working through the emotional wreckage that keeps them from reaching them. It's very gratifying. What a great sense of satisfaction we receive from the act of giving to others from whom we ask nothing in the way of payment.

In many cases, maybe most, the richness of the rewards of helping these people who can't pay us for doing it even transcends the joy of seeing people grow in our courses in companies who pay us.

New Paradigms of Thought About the Causes of Organizational Success

Organizations and individuals are in a constant state of transformation and renewal; hence such terms as "reinventing" and "reengineering." Many of these fixes du jour were not necessarily wrong; they were just misdirected. While all of us, individually and corporately, have a need for introspection, self-examination, and process improvement, when that becomes our aim, it can weaken us. The technological craze of the seventies and eighties along with the reorganizational mania of the nineties, gives testimony to this belief.

Shannon O'Connell, writing in *Data Management Review*, recently wrote

> After a decade of downsizing, corporations are beginning to feel the effects of severe cost-cutting. Virtually every department in downsized corporations is realizing the burden of a decimated employee work force.

She quotes an *American Management* survey that showed that 49 percent of downsized organizations showed no increase in profitability, and productivity rose in only 39 percent. But the real kicker was that employee morale slumped 86 percent.

But everything is action and reaction. So after three decades of flattened productivity we dig for new, more significant answers.

Today, we hear a common cry from many quarters. A cry that attempts to get at the core of the productivity problem. The cry is for values, ethics, integrity, authenticity, character—old-fashioned values that somehow got lost in the structural shuffle of the last few decades.

In the last decade or so, we've seen our business heroes' feet of clay exposed and crumpled. The Ivan Boeskys, Michael Milkins, Charles Keatings gave testimony to the grim reality that there are forces in life that correct the imbalances of the excessive takers.

My favorite philosopher (You'd never have guessed it, would you?) wrote in his essay on "Compensation"

> There is always some leveling circumstance that puts down the overbearing, the strong, the rich, the fortunate, substantially on the same ground with all others.

A perfect equity adjusts its balance in all parts of life. The dice of God are always loaded.

Every secret is told, every crime is punished, every virtue rewarded, every wrong redressed, in silence and certainty.

Every act rewards itself, or in other words, integrates itself in a two-fold manner; first in the thing or in real nature; and secondly in the circumstance or apparent nature.

Cause and effect, means and ends, seeds and fruit, cannot be severed; for the effect already blooms in the cause, the end pre-exists in the means, the fruit in the seed.

Now, please hang with me because this isn't the end of our journey together. The following truth is vital to this book.

Our Beliefs Are Powerful in Influencing Others

The one overwhelming thread I see running through all the vicissitudes or changes in business in the last quadrillion years is that the prevailing beliefs of leaders translate themselves into their tangible equivalent in organizations.

Think about it. When leaders believed that profit was most important, that got translated into all the policies and strategies of their businesses. When they thought that process, technology, organizational structure, customer satisfaction, or loyalty were most important—all these focuses predestined certain effects.

Charles Elliot once remarked, "All business proceeds on beliefs, or judgments of probabilities, and not on certainties."

Yes, leaders' beliefs are so powerful that they are translated into reality. Someone said once, "Be careful what you believe because that belief will get carried out in your life and into the lives of those you influence."

Let's think about the power of beliefs. Then I'll challenge

you to carefully select specific beliefs you have, or think you should have, and run them through the litmus test of cause and effect.

"Believe that life is worth living," wrote William James, the father of modern-day psychology, "and your belief will help create the fact."

What a powerful, stimulating thought.

Could Dr. James be speaking about the same *transcending* power that Thomas Watson Jr. spoke of in the opening of this chapter?

B. C. Forbes, in his writings advised, "Believe in yourself, your neighbors, your work, your ultimate attainment of more complete happiness." Let's use his advice and apply it to some very practical applications in your business.

Expectations Are Projected Beliefs About Your People

Your expectations, what you unconsciously think that each of your people is *capable* of producing and *will* produce, are powerful beliefs that are telepathically sent out to them. You *project* these beliefs in your actions, attitudes, and behaviors. Unconsciously you say, "I expect you to perform at a high level and be able to do a superior job." Or you may project, "I expect low performance out of you and don't see you rising above certain levels."

Your every action supports your belief. The way you look at people, greet them, your tone of voice, the things you talk about—all these carry your message about what you believe about them and what you expect from them. You can't hide it. You will communicate your true feelings, and it will go straight to their "I Am" dimension.

Your people will pick up your beliefs about them and your evaluation of them. They may consciously notice it in your behavior, or they may get it through subliminal channels in their "I Am." But they'll get it!

And when they get your message, they'll process it some-thing like this: "Here's what the boss thinks of me. Now, she's a smart person and must be right; therefore, I must be what she thinks I am."

Certainly in a much more subtle manner and language than I've just used, but it's played and replayed until the self-belief is set.

Remember the Law of Limited Performance? It was

> People soon discover the level of performance that their managers will settle for and gravitate to that level. Managers then assume that's all that people are capable of achieving, so they accept it as fact and quit challenging their people to get better. So, each reinforces what the other believes.

Examine this law and you'll conclude that much (maybe even most) of people's performance is simply the result of beliefs. Their beliefs about who they are and what they're capable of producing; your beliefs and expectations about them and their capabilities; their beliefs and expectations about your beliefs and expectations.

Beliefs That Positively Influence Your People

As we emphasize the power of a leader's beliefs, let's look at your:

1. Belief in the purpose of your organization.
2. Belief in the integrity of your management team.
2. Belief in your ability to carry out your part of your organization's mission and results.
4. Belief in your people's ability to achieve the goals they commit to reach.

5. Belief that your beliefs will reproduce themselves after their kind.

Now, since I've either written about or alluded to the first four, let me land on the fifth one: Believing that your beliefs will reproduce themselves after their kind.

Over time, much has been written about the power of belief. There is an ongoing evolution of thought and an expansion of knowledge, so our ability to understand and explain belief changes. The evolution has gone from being a religious and spiritual context, to a more mystical one. It's as if we discover facets of truth that move us in a certain direction, then another, and another.

As our paradigms expand and different facets are combined in order to explain a congruence or harmony of the different "truths" or beliefs, we are forced to explore different areas. In the last few years, it's been the spiritual beliefs that have come to the forefront of study. Now, don't cut me off just because I've used the word "spiritual" because this has direct impact on your role of leader, whatever you do.

A 1996 *Time* magazine article titled, "Faith and Healing" asked the question, "Can spirituality promote health?" A Time/CNN poll conducted by Yankelovich Partners, Inc., revealed the following results from 1,004 American adults. When asked, "Do you believe in

1. "The healing power of prayer?" yes-82%; no-13%
2. "That praying for someone else can help cure their illness?" yes-73%; no-21%
3. "God sometimes intervenes to cure people who have a serious illness?" yes-77%; no-18%
4. "In the ability of faith healers to make people well through their faith or personal touch?" yes-28%; no-63%
5. "Doctors should join their patients in prayer if the patients request it?" yes-64%; no-27%

Interesting ideas that people have about belief.

I mentioned Dr. Herbert Benson's book, *Timeless Healing*, earlier. Benson is the author of the popular seventies book *Relaxation Response* and associate professor of medicine at Harvard University Medical School. In his newer book, he makes some startling cases about the power of belief in physical healing. Let's consider a few of his medical-research findings and then see if they translate into some realities that impact your getting more done through people.

Let me begin by quoting Dr. Benson's beginning premise. He writes,

> I am convinced that our bodies are wired to benefit from exercising not only our muscles but our rich inner human core—our beliefs, values, thoughts, and feelings. I was reluctant to explore these factors because philosophers and scientists have, through the ages, considered them intangible and unmeasurable, making any study of them 'unscientific.'
>
> But I wanted to try because again and again my patients' progress and recoveries often seemed to hinge upon their spirit and will to live. And I could not shake the sense I had that the human mind—and the beliefs we so often associate with the human soul—had physical manifestations.

Now, let's pause a moment and get on the same page. Yes, I know you're probably not a medical doctor. I know that you are a manager charged with getting tangible results. You have to deal in the real world and make stuff happen. I know all that.

Dr. Benson points out that in addition to exercising your muscles and mind, it's also important to exercise your beliefs, values, thoughts, and feelings. What an interesting thought.

"Beliefs have physical manifestations," he emphasizes. The physical manifestation of your beliefs is your people's productivity—what they get done. Your beliefs about your organization's purpose, about the integrity of your management team, about your ability to carry out your part of your organization's mission, about your people's ability to achieve the goal they commit to reach, and your beliefs about how much your beliefs will reproduce themselves after their kind. It's these beliefs that will powerfully influence your productivity. You and your people can have great knowledge, skills, processes, and technology, but you will never reach the highest level of productivity possible without the power of beliefs that I'm describing.

I realize that this paradigm runs smack up against conventional wisdom. You can't see it, or measure it, or in many cases, even prove it. Reason and logic don't necessarily apply here.

A timeless truth is that faith and belief tend to transcend knowledge. In the business world we need to frame everything in reality. Once our beliefs are labeled or framed, we don't see through our perceived reality. But belief and faith don't fit those frames that we carefully design around our logical lives, so we don't challenge our assumptions. We don't grow. We stay in our cultivated comfort zones.

Try This Experiment

If you want to test the power of your people's beliefs in influencing the actions, feelings, and behavior of other people, try the following experiment.

First, line up six to eight people in a straight line, standing abreast, facing you. Have them put their right arms around the people to their right and stand close together. Test the arm strength of both people on the two ends just to get a feel for their natural strength.

Then whisper to a person in the line to think of a positive, happy event that he or she recently experienced. Ask the person to dwell mentally on that event. Then test the arm strength of the two people on the ends of the line. You'll notice that it is very strong in proportion to their actual natural strength.

Then whisper to a person in the line to think of a recent

negative experience and to dwell on it as vividly as he or she can. Again, check the arm strength of the two end people. This time, you'll notice that they've lost almost all of their previous strength. It will shock them.

The lesson is that the person's thoughts, be they negative or positive, are immediately transferred to the other people.

If you really want to see some amazing reactions, ask a person (so no one hears what you're telling them) to think or say thoughts like

"I like me!"
"I don't like me!"
"One thing I like about (name a person) is _____."
"One thing I *don't* like about (name a person) is _____."
"I see good in everyone!"
"Everyone's just out for themselves."
"What I do has purpose and significance."
"I'm just here to put in my time."
"I like and trust my coworkers."
"I don't like or trust my coworkers."

Test the arm strength of two of the people in the line after each statement has been said.

When you do this exercise, you'll discover an interconnectedness among your people. You'll see that the thoughts of one person influence the strength and energy of the others. You'll be blown away by the commonality of people, the subliminal communication that takes place even when they don't consciously know what the other people are thinking.

A Whole New Level of Communication

In the preceding experiment, you'll discover a whole new level of communication between people. One that operates in a totally different realm than what our linear, logical minds have been trained to understand.

As you do this experiment, you'll develop some new paradigms of thought and understanding about the power of people's beliefs in influencing others.

Here are some things you'll learn.

1. Whatever people choose to think about is immediately, though subliminally, picked up by people around them.

2. When people think negative, destructive thoughts, they project them to others, weakening the strength and energy of others.

3. When people think positive, constructive thoughts, they project them to others, strengthening the energy of others.

4. Your thoughts about your possibilities, your people, their potential, your organization's value—all are transferred to your people. These then cause people to be energized or weakened.

5. Your thoughts influence your realities.

So, be very watchful about the thoughts you think, because what you send out is going to influence what you can get done through people.

Choosing What Thoughts You Want to Send Out

Understanding the power of your own thoughts and beliefs to influence your own and other people's energy and productive capacity is a sobering concept. We know so little of this power. Partly because we dismiss the whole concept as "spooky," "mystical," or "New Age." What we don't understand, we tend to ignore or discredit. But wise people have known about this for centuries. Two thousand years ago, the Apostle Paul, writing the Book of Philippians, gave this advice about how to have a more abundant life. He wrote:

> "... whatever is true, whatever is honorable, whatever is right, whatever is pure, whatever is lovely, whatever is of good repute, if there is any excellence and if anything worthy of praise, let your mind dwell on these things."

This is great advice for focusing on what is wholesome, productive and upbuilding. It is also psychologically sound.

Yes, not only do we become what we think about, but we also get back from people the same responses as the thoughts we send out to them.

So, understanding the power of your own beliefs gives credence and power to these Basic Values and Beliefs.

1. People have unlimited potential.
2. People are intrinsically good.
3. People return to us the same attitudes and responses we give them.
4. People deeply yearn for significance and meaning.
5. People respond to positive leadership.
6. People feel better about themselves when they take responsibility and keep commitments.

When you internalize these beliefs and project them to others in your thoughts and interactions, you'll positively influence others.

Integrity Adds Power to Your Beliefs

Integrity. Interesting word. We use it a lot. In fact, that's the name of my organization: Integrity Systems® We market among other things a course called *Integrity Selling®*.

Integrity means several things: completeness, wholeness, uprightness, honesty, sincerity. It's when the inner is integrated with the outer; what you see is what you get.

I believe that in the scheme of things, integrity increases power. It liberates, it reduces drag or negative restrictions. It energizes and synergizes.

The power of belief is made stronger by the extent to which it is spawned out of integrity. Sincerity, conviction, positive passion—all strengthen the power of belief.

Summing Up

"Belief and philosophy," Thomas J. Watson Jr. said, "constitute a transcendent factor which outweighs technology, economic resources, or anything else, in achieving success."

Belief, the power of belief in impacting your people's productivity, is this chapter's message.

I've challenged you to have new views of the power of your beliefs. Belief is neither logical nor quantifiable. It's emotional and even spiritual. Our beliefs are communicated through our expectations.

Belief in the possibility of positive outcomes and in the inherent worth of people forms a powerful chemical catalyst that multiplies the sum of people's knowledge, skills, and technology to form a new strength, one that influences profitability and effectiveness. That's my message to you in this chapter.

I know that this tends to fly in the face of conventional wisdom; of logical, rational, you-gotta-prove-it-to-me kind of thinking. The very kind of bottom-line thinking that has to be done in order to manage things. Yeah, I know that. I run a business, so I know you have to be logical.

All great leaders either intuitively or consciously understand this power and have integrated it into their actions. That's why they're great leaders.

The same can work for you.

How to Gain the Most from This Chapter

Read this chapter and select three or four major thoughts that speak loudest to you.

Ask yourself, "If the thoughts I send out influence my people's responses, behaviors, and productivity, then what specific results do I want and what thoughts can I send out that will tend to engineer those results?"

Make a list of these thoughts on index cards. Carry them, read them several times daily, and project those thoughts to others.

Make and read statements like these.

1. "I believe in the purpose of my organization."
2. "I believe in the integrity of my management team."
3. "I believe in my ability to carry out my part of my organization's mission and results."
4. "I believe in my people's ability to reach the goals they commit to reach."
5. "I believe that my beliefs will reproduce themselves after their kind."

Write down, read, and repeat to yourself several times each day what William James wrote

"Believe that life is worth living, and your belief will cause the fact."

Yes, beliefs help create realities.

Afterword

In this book, I've shared what I've discovered and learned over many years about what causes human action and performance.

I've been blessed with unbelievable success, far surpassing what I ever thought possible. I am truly thankful to the Creator and to our million and a half course graduates and over nineteen thousand facilitators who have been certified to conduct my courses. That I could have touched the lives of that many people certainly bears witness of Help that's beyond what I could have done myself.

In this book, I have shared some very practical models, strategies, and ideas that will strengthen your leadership skills. But, as I wrote in the first chapter, simply practicing these ideas will surely help you increase your own personal *leadership abilities*, but they won't necessarily make you a *leader*.

It's only when you add that "something else" that you will become a leader.

In every chapter I have led you through thought processes and action guides that if you practiced and learned helped you discover that "something else." Clues about what this magic ingredient, this chemical catalyst, is have been continually dropped for you to stumble over, dig up, and examine.

I said that I would not tell you directly what this "something else" is. That thrill is reserved for you to dig out and put together in your own framework of thinking. Because you have searched for it and broadened your thinking, it will indeed become your discovery to celebrate and put into your bank account of wisdom and knowledge.

Discovering this "something else," as you'll find, is a lifelong search, peeling off layer after layer of discovery.

So, my best to you. I'm thrilled that our lives have come together through this book. I'm excited about your application of the concepts in this book.

May you enjoy the serendipity of prosperity, fulfillment, and abundance as you *help people become their best.*